INTRODUCTION
Sinclair Gauldie

Dundee's architectural character defeats any attempt to evaluate it by comparison with the other Scottish cities. The eighteenth-century burgh never experienced that expansion of a civilised middle-class which ensured the success of Edinburgh's New Town, nor did subsequent generations possess the great resources and fierce determination which stamped an ordered gridiron plan across the intractable contours of Victorian Glasgow. Unlike Aberdeen, its closest parallel, Dundee's nineteenth-century wealth was not built out of the harvests of the hinterland and the fishing grounds, but out of the exertions of a resident proletariat: and the need for housing (and subsequently re-housing) that proletariat and its descendants has largely moulded the city's shape over the past 150 years. Patrick Geddes, who took a lively interest in Dundee's social problems during his professorship there, identified the interaction of "place, work, folk" as the determinant of the form of any human settlement, and perhaps the aphorism was inspired by his connection with a city which so vividly illustrates that interaction: as the son of one of his students at University College, Dundee, I would like to think so.

Take first the place: an estuarial harbour separated from southern Scotland by a two-mile width of tidal waterway and blocked-off by the Sidlaw Hills from fertile Strathmore and the historical main route to the north: enjoying a micro-climate which is kinder than on most of the east coast and drier than most of the west: founded on a rather coarse kind of sedimentary rock thinly overlaid with stony clay and punctuated by volcanic outcrops. Such a place was likely, from earliest history, to raise a breed of people who sense themselves to be physically somewhat detached from the other centres of population and to look out to sea rather than towards the hinterland for contacts, trade and opportunities: a people whose tradition will be to build with local stone and imported timber rather than brick and to employ an architectural vernacular based on those materials and coloured by influences from other countries on the maritime trade routes.

Second, the work. Fishing and shipbuilding were natural occupations in such a place. The first was carried on in a modest way from the

Anthony:
It is shap'd, sir, like itself,
and it is as broad as it hath
breadth; it is just so high as
it is. . . .

Lepidus:
What colour is it of?

Anthony:
Of its own colour too.
Anthony and Cleopatra II. vii.

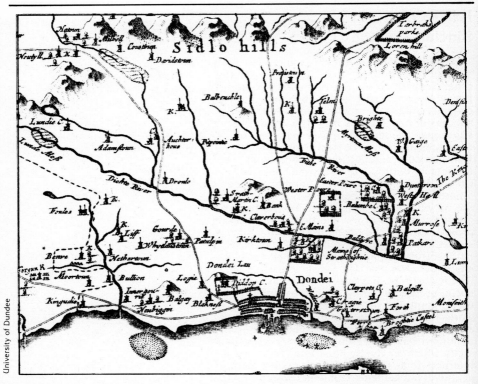

Dundee and Angus in the late 17th
century, showing the strategic position at
the Firth of Tay.

University of Dundee

earliest times until the Second World War,
reaching its apogee with the Arctic whalers of
the nineteenth century: shipbuilding also
reached its peak before 1914 but survived,
with a high reputation for quality, until very
recent years. Mercantile seafaring was an
equally natural occupation, and the contacts
which it established were to put Dundee firmly
on the road to becoming a single-industry
town, a condition which was to have far-
reaching and indelible effects upon its
architectural character.

Among those contacts were the
entrepreneurs of the flourishing woollen
industry of Flanders, who were not only
trading through the east coast ports for their
raw material but by the twelfth century were
being encouraged to settle and put their
capital and skill to use here in Britain. To
them is generally given the credit for
establishing the textile industry which was to
be a conspicuous and eventually a dominant
component of the Dundee economy from the
Middle Ages onward: and, once established,
this expertise in the making and marketing of
textiles earned the eighteenth-century burgh a

2

reputation for the production of coarse linens which was to last throughout the next century: Baxters' sailcloth went into action at Trafalgar and covered the waggons which opened up the American West, and Macgregor's firehoses safeguarded the early New York skyscrapers.

Coarse linen led to jute, a transition made possible by the use of the batching-oil so conveniently procurable in a whaling port; with the growth of the textile industry arose an engineering industry to supply it and to serve the shipbuilders, creating yet another tradition of inventiveness, expertise and craftmanship and one which survives the transition from heavy to light engineering.

Thirdly, the folk. Surely the most striking fact about the Dundonians is that there are so many of them. Given its geographical isolation and its early historical misfortunes (culminating in the Cromwellian massacre of 1651) there would have been no good reason for Dundee to grow bigger than, say, Perth. In fact, the population of 26,000 in 1801 had increased sixfold by the end of the century, even before Broughty Ferry (which had grown correspondingly) was incorporated in the city. This expansion was not, of course, the product of natural increase alone: it was the result of massive immigration, first from Angus, Perthshire and the Highlands, then from Ireland, in response to the labour demands of the textile industry. Moreover, the effect of the explosion was not only quantitative but qualitative. A modest burgh with a fairly typical eighteenth-century social stratification, whose "tone" was set by the life-styles of merchants and skilled artisans, became within a matter of decades an industrial city with an overwhelmingly proletarian population: and a great proportion of that population were first-generation peasant immigrants with no tradition of city living and no long-standing attachment to the place of their exile: regarded by the original natives as cheap imported labour (capable of paying only minimal rents) their needs for homes was seen not as the basis for a new pattern of urban settlement — a New Lanark or Saltaire or Siemensstadt — but simply as a problem of storage, and an urgent one. The response to that problem created the bulk of Dundee's building stock, and explains the scarcity of architectural survivals from the medieval and eighteenth-century burgh as well as the absence of examples of the kind of up-market street design which gave the New Town of Edinburgh "its essential character of public

THREE DUNDEE ARCHITECTS

JAMES BLACK (a Whig) arrived in Dundee in 1817 and eventually ousted David Neave (the Tory) as the Town's Architect after the downfall of the Provost Riddoch faction; but he failed to attract work and built little, spending most of his time embroiled in terrible scrimmages over competitions.

J. M. ROBERTSON, a strict Plymouth Brother, was to become one of Dundee's most distinctive native architects. He had come to Dundee with Andrew Heiton of Perth to design the mansion Castleroy in Broughty Ferry, for the Gilroy family. He suited them to the extent that they encouraged him to begin practice on his own. Robertson was initially deeply influenced by Alexander (Greek) Thomson, (see India Buildings, Bell Street), and then by American prototypes, particularly the mid-west architect H. H. Richardson. From these examples derived his innovations — the use of mass concrete and flat detailing. From Dundee, his leitmotif became projecting, flattened bays capped by ogee roofs, clearly based on the Morgan Tower (see p. 60). The practice mutated through Robertson and Findlay; then Findlay, Stewart and Robbie; to the current office of Robbie and Wellwood.

JAMES THOMSON was an extraordinarily able man beyond being the father of two architects, Harry and Frank. After a spell in the office of the City Engineer, he succeeded Alexander as City Architect in 1904 and Mackison as City Engineer in 1906. His reputation — leaving aside that earned by the *mystery house* and by helping his sons — is based upon his development plan for Dundee which was far ahead of its time. Alongside the positive proposals for a northern by-pass (Kingsway), a

3

garden city for the working class (the Craigie estate) and a new purpose designed elephantine Civic Centre on the site of Earl Grey Dock (a fitting irony that Tayside Regional Council occupies a commercial office block on virtually the same site 60 years later); to him might also be credited the invention of the road-widening safeguarding line, (which destroys townscape by requiring new buildings to be set back); the destruction of William Adam's Town House (although his plan did include a variant showing how it could be saved), the first peripheral housing estate, and the proposals to eliminate the historic character of old Dundee (eg Seagate) by road widening. It was to Thomson's credit that, in Logie, Dundee built the first-ever district heated housing scheme.

below: The Kail Kirk (see p. 34).

grandeur based on private restraint".

Up to the eighteenth century, a very high proportion of Dundee's houses seem to have been timber-built, to the extent that it was found necessary at one time to legislate against timber chimneys. The sacking of the burgh by Monk's troops must have put paid to many of these, though some survived long enough to figure in Victorian pictures. Their successors tended to be built in stone with slated roofs, tall and often with narrow street frontages and entrances off a wynd or close. The earlier of these were among the first casualties of the population explosion. Once the more prosperous burghers dispersed to the suburbs out of range of the proliferating mill-stalks, the houses of eighteenth-century burgesses and country lairds, given over to multiple occupancy, degenerated by degrees into overcrowded and ill-maintained rookeries. By the time it became fashionable to admire and preserve such reminders of the vernacular tradition, most of them had either become practically irredeemable or had been swept away by the exigencies of street widening. The town's traffic pattern, funnelling from all directions into the nexus formed by the markets and the harbour, eventually put an intolerable stress on the narrow central streets and the inevitable clearances not only swept away much of the old housing stock but destroyed the eighteenth-century public buildings which, complementing the Town House, had provided the town with a formal and relatively urbane focus for assemblies of all kinds, from Hogmanays to hangings.

The diaspora of the better-heeled bourgeoisie had both direct and indirect consequences, the most interesting of these being the inflation of Broughty Ferry from a fishing hamlet to a plutocratic satellite, a municipality in its own right complete with Town Council and Provost. Not only was this satellite an architectural phenomenon in its own right but it had a curious indirect effect upon Dundee. One Victorian Town Clerk, looking back over his experience, lamented the absence from civic affairs of the "men of substance" who ought to be playing a major part in them: the energy and acumen which had so enlarged the city's industry could surely have contributed to its wellbeing. The absence of such a contribution he put down to the fact that many of those men no longer lived within the burgh boundaries; and this in turn he ascribed largely to the opening of the Dundee-Arbroath railway and the consequent facility of setting-up house in Broughty Ferry, where a taste for municipal politics could be indulged in more congenial surroundings.

Be that as it may, it is a fact that the population explosion posed problems which would have taxed minds of a much higher calibre than those then available in the Town House. The application of steam power to the linen industry had already created a housing shortage and the problem ballooned with the advent of jute. Even if the city fathers had considered this to be a matter for their attention — a doubtful supposition, given the *laissez-faire* climate of the time — they had, by 1840, become involved in a prolonged course of futile litigation over water rights and ministers' stipends which resulted in the burgh's finances being removed from their control and placed for several years in charge of public trustees. Both the power and the pride of the Town Council must have been sadly shaken in the middle of the century and although the industrialists of that period were short of neither power nor pride — their ' factory architecture sometimes bore striking witness to the latter — their contribution on the housing front was minimal. The financing of cheaply-rented housing was not attractive to men whose capital could be far more profitably deployed upon their manufacturing operations or in the exploitation of the American connection which had originated with the supply of loosely-woven linen to the cotton plantations and would eventually mortgage many a Texan ranch to Dundee-based investment trusts.

The tenements which grew up around the mills were predominantly the piecemeal creation of small-scale developers, generally builders or house factors, and a high proportion consisted of one or two-apartment flats: it was almost as if the but-and-ben cottages familiar to rural immigrants were set on top of one another instead of end-to-end. No more in the one case than in the other did it seem outrageous to have the privy outside the back door, a fact which greatly simplified and cheapened the design of the flat, but left subsequent generations with problems. The walling material of the tenement blocks came almost entirely from local quarries. A freestone of variable quality, prone to flaking if badly selected or carelessly built, it boasts neither the sparkle of Aberdeen granite nor the austere crispness of Craigleith. It shows to best advantage in bluntly-detailed domestic work and can disastrously betray its humble

above: The Tay Hotel and the shore.
below: The Camperdown Works.

Wishart

The Mercat Cross of Dundee 1586 (see p. 54).

origins by delaminating where elaborately wrought — especially if quarried from the most accessible, and hence cheapest, beds. In short, an essentially homely stone, curiously appropriate to a town whose folk are never slow to mock the pretentious.

By the end of the 1880's, the boom in tenement and mill building was over, but, within a generation, rising expectations — especially in the field of public health — were creating a peripheral belt of new housing as the municipality (now seized of the problem, empowered by Acts of Parliament and ably served by ambitious executives) dealt first with the last residues of the pre-industrial slums and then with the worst of the Victorian heritage. At the same time, an enlarging middle class were becoming suburban house-owners instead of tenants of city tenements and terraces; and as the traditional industry declined, manufacturing also moved out to the periphery.

Today, the wheel is coming full circle, with the emphasis on the rehabilitation and reclamation of the nineteenth-century precincts and the return of industry to the inner city. A land-use map of Dundee in 1930 would have shown dereliction at the core and new growth on the fringes, the classic pattern of urban deterioration. That has changed, but such a map even today reads like a section through a tree-trunk, in which the seeing eye can trace the vicissitudes of the organism, its good seasons and bad seasons, from the time it was a sapling. And this, in fact, is how the architectural history of this city can most profitably be studied. The pleasure of it is not in the instant response to the grand set-piece or to the comfortably quaint. It is more like the fascination of the historical detective-story: the unfolding, layer by layer, of the interactions of place, work and folk over a thousand years. So complicated have these interactions been, and so inextricable is fact from myth in the histories of the city, that its architectural anatomy has never been comprehensively studied with the accuracy which it deserves and probably never can be. This present account of it by Charles McKean is certainly the most ambitious to date, and makes a useful introduction to a city which has always exemplified not only Geddes' aphorism but the words of the most famous of its Members of Parliament: *We make our buildings and they make us.*

Sinclair Gauldie

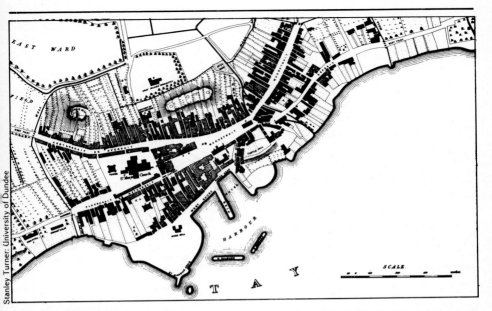

THE TOWN PLAN

Central Dundee in 1776, the plan clearly illustrating Edward's anatomical analogy: a man on his back, his arms and legs outstretched, the belly in the market place.

Dundee, squeezed between the Law and the Tay, has a town plan best described by analogy, never put better than in 1678 by the Rev. Robert Edward, Minister of Murroes, and father of Sir William Bruce's amanuensis: *The town is divided into four principal streets, which we may suppose to represent a human body, stretched on its back with its arms towards the west, and its legs towards the east. The steeple represents the head, with an enormous neck, rising upwards of eighteen storeys, into the clouds and surrounded with two battlements or galleries, one in the middle, and another at the top, like a crown adorning the head-whose loud-sounding tongue daily calls the people to worship. The right hand is stretched forth to the poor, for there is a large and well-furnished hospital on that side; but the left hand, because nearer to the heart, is more elevated towards heaven than the right-indicating a devout mind panting after celestial joys. In the inmost recesses of the breast stand the sacred temples of God. On the left breast is a Christian burying-place, richly and piously ornamented, that the pious dead may be long held in veneration and esteem. In the belly is the market-place, at the middle of which is the "cross" like the navel in the body. Below the loins stand the shambles, which, as they are in a proper place, so are they very neat and convenient, having a hidden stream of fresh water, which (after wandering*

HISTORIC DUNDEE from the north. c 1670. One of the two earliest drawings of Dundee, by Captain John Slezer. It shows a substantial port and market town, with a considerable number of significant stone buildings. The Scots historian Sibbald, who contributed the descriptions for Slezer's drawings recorded a town *adorned with excellent buildings of all sorts. It hath two churches, a high steeple, a harbour for ships of burthen, and a considerable traffic with strangers, whence the inhabitants are generally rich, and those who fall into decay have a large hospital provided for them.*

through the pleasant meadows on the left), runs under them; and which having thus, as it were, scoured the veins and intestines of the town, is afterwards discharged into the river. Here the thighs and legs are separated. The sea approaching the right, invites to the trade and commerce of foreign countries; and the left limb, separated from the thigh a full step, points to home trade, in the northern parts of the country. This book begins with a topographical stroll around the torso and legs of the old City: beginning with the belly (High Street), moving to the right thigh at Castle Street to the Shore, following that to the extremities of the two legs of Cowgate and Seagate; then returning up the body to the head, at the Auld Steeple, to follow the right ear out the Nethergate. That is followed by three detailed sections covering the University precinct, Magdalen Yard and Chapelshade. The description of outer Dundee follows the radial routes, taken clockwise.

Thomas Morer, an army chaplain, had visited the town four years earlier, to be *handsomely treated at the charges of the corporation;* in gratitude for which he recorded *a very pretty town at the bottom of a hill . . . furnished with two or three small piers for the conveniency of shipping, and the buildings are such as speak the substance and riches of the place.*

Details and Access

Buildings are generally listed in the order of name, address, architect (designer if known) and date. The usual date given is that of design. Although many of the buildings described are public and easily accessible, many are private and their inclusion implies no right of access. Users are asked to respect the privacy of the owners and other users.

These optimistic descriptions are at variance with the contemporary records of the poverty which struck Dundee after its sacking by General Monk in 1651. It is said that with the possible exception of Drogheda, no town suffered so much in the Civil War. Many people had sent their goods for safekeeping to Dundee. Monk attacked the town at a time when, according to Sir James Balfour, *the townes men were most of them drunken, lyke so many beasts.* Dr Gumble, General Monk's biographer, wrote that both soldiers and townsfolk *took such large Morning draughts that before the Twelfth (hour) they were most of them well drenched in their cups.* Both are probably *post hoc facto* justification of the fact that the town was sacked and many hundreds of soldiers and civilians slaughtered. Some 60 vessels were captured, providing a booty of, it is said, over £50 sterling per soldier in Monk's army; *the best plunder* according to Gumble, *that was gotten in the Wars throughout the three nations.* Thomas Tucker, Register to the Commissioner for the Excise in England ventured north in 1655 to report on various Scots ports, with little sympathy for the Royalist rebels: *The towne of Dundee was sometimes a towne of riches and trade, but the many recontres it hath mett withall in the time*

above: Dundee from the river in the 18th century. The tree-lined walk from the shore up to the centre of town, recorded by Daniel Defoe is clearly visible. The great Castle hill is on the right behind the masts.

Give me leave wrote the English Captain Richard Franck in 1656 *to call it deplorable Dundee; and not to be exprest without a deluge of tears; because storm'd and spoil'd by the rash precipitancy of mercenaries whose rapinous hands put a fatal period to her stately embellishments . . . Ah, poor Dundee! torn up by the roots; and thy natives and inhabitants pick't out at the portholes. Blush, O heavens, what an age is this! There was wealth enough to answer their ambitions, and probably that as soon as any thing betrayed her.* In a more prosaic vein he also noticed the town's *beautiful parts* and the *embodied mists to which Dundee is incident as any part, because standing in a bottom that's beseiged with mucky, miry earth; from whence there insurrect such pernicious vapours as nauseate the air. . . .*

9

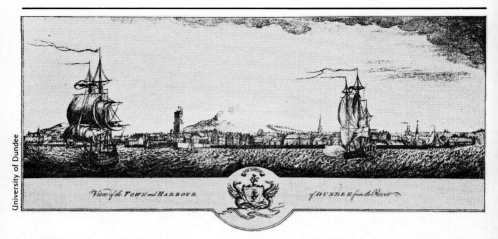

View of the TOWN and HARBOUR.

of DUNDEE from the River.

DUNDEE from the river in the 18th century:
This vignette from Crawford's map, shows the first experience of Dundee for most visitors as they travelled from Fife by ferry. The town is penned between Corbie Hill and the sea leading to a very extenuated east-west layout. To the left is the Town Hospital. The Old Steeple retains its predominance but it is now being jostled by the tower of William Adam's Town House, and Samuel Bell's new St Andrew's Church (p. 40) on the right.

of Domestick comotions, and her obstinacy and pride of late years, rendering her prey to the soldier, have much shaken and abated her former grandeur; and not withstanding all, shee remaynes still, though not glorious, yet not contemptible.

The economic consequences of the sack were exacerbated by a ferocious storm in 1658: the harbour was damaged and remained ruinous for almost 20 years, during which period the council frequently had to distribute free oat meal to alleviate starvation. Slezer's two views show a considerable town with a fine harbour. But they also illustrate an underpopulated town, with plentiful space and gardens; a town without the high, densely packed buildings of contemporary Edinburgh or Stirling; a town of substantial merchant's houses, but generally lacking the grand buildings visible in his views of Glasgow or Old Aberdeen. Indeed, apart from the Old Steeple, there are few features of notice: the Castle Rock is clearly visible rising from the harbour; a small, turreted house can be faintly discerned to the East of the steeple, being the ruinous Tolbooth later to be replaced by William Adam's Town House, (p. 14); and to the west of the spire is a large building with projecting wings and a tower at the centre (which by 1776 had been capped by a cupola). That was the *Town's Hospital,* now demolished. Founded in 1567, the hospital stood at the foot of South Tay Street, and was burned in 1645. The rebuilt Hospital was, in 1678 *a large and splendid hospital for old men,* an opinion supported by Daniel Defoe in 1726 who thought it a *handsome hospital, with the garden running down to the river.* It was vacated in 1746, used for French prisoners of war and then as a Grammar School, eventually to be replaced by the Catholic Cathedral (see p. 57). Dudhope Castle (p. 71) can be seen on the right of the Slezer view, with a strong, seemingly fifteenth-century battlement tower, subsequently removed.

TENDALL'S WYND: this sixteenth-century building, now demolished, gives a fair idea of the better-off Dundee merchant's houses prior to the industrial revolution. Unlike the grand tenement buildings of Edinburgh and Glasgow, the merchant houses tended to be individual houses; not flatted. A protruding circular stairway, sometimes capped by a turret, was not uncommon. There was some sculptural elaboration, but not to a significant degree; everything being rather more plain and businesslike. The owners of this property, Auchinleck, are commemorated by a curious tombstone in the Howff. The late seventeenth-century historian Ochterlony, sets the context of such buildings: *Dundee is a large and great town, very populous, and of a great trade, and hath many good ships. The buildings are large and great, of thrie or four stories high; a large market place with a very fine tolbuith and cross; two great churches, with a very high steeple well furnished of bells. . . . It lyeth upon the Water of Tay very pleasantlie and hath great yards and meadows about it. . . .*

PROVOST PIERSON'S MANSION.
According to the architectural historians MacGibbon and Ross, the Pierson building in the Greenmarket, was *one of the most remarkable specimens of a town house left in Scotland which, with care might have lasted for centuries to come.* The continuous ground floor arcading was originally full height, and unusually sophisticated example of an arcaded building in Scotland. It predated 1640. Rather similar arcading is to be seen on the inner face of the west wall of the Howff; almost certainly put up by the same hand.

STRATHMARTINE'S LODGING, whose location is commemorated by a beautiful relief panel inside the City Chambers, was an unusual example of an early eighteenth-century landowner's hôtel, with a fine projecting octagonal staircase and ogival roof. The neatly shaped gable and other details were Dutch in influence.

Dundee District Libraries

above: Provost Pierson's mansion, now demolished. The corner towers would originally have had conical roofs. *below:* The Strathmartine lodging. *below left:* Tendall's Wynd.

McKean: from Lamb's Dundee

The country squires wrote an anonymous commentator in 1799, *have, for the present, quitted the town . . . they find that self consequences and self importance are delicate and tender plants, that are much more quietly reared and nursed in wilds and heaths, and amongst mountains and forests than in the bustling circle of a mercantile and independent community.*

¹ **DUNDEE MARKET AND HIGH STREET.** This is the centre of old Dundee, and the view above, in 1845 shows it at what was probably the City's architectural peak. Major new Civic buildings had been constructed, new streets had been opened leading to other public buildings — Reform Street to the north leading to the High School; and Castle Street to the South leading to the Docks and the Exchange Coffee House. Suburbs of late eighteenth-century Mansions and early nineteenth-century villas lay to the east, west and north and Dundee's few classical urban designs had been built — western Nethergait, Tay Street, Union Street, Reform Street and King Street. The core of late mediaeval and sixteenth/seventeenth-century merchants homes still survived, not yet so totally

abandoned into the slums that they were to become. In short, central Dundee was bursting with civic pride, even though its persistant encouragement of individualism made it the only significant community in nineteenth-century Scotland to forego large-scale classical replanning. All the major buildings facing the High Street have now been replaced. The oldest, on the corner of Overgate, was a sixteenth/seventeenth-century tenement with a truncated turret: the building in which General Monk rested after his massacre.

This view of the High Street shows: the **TOWN HOUSE** on the left; and the **UNION HALL** closing the vista, demonstrating, wrote a commentator *much of that opulent and commercially great and dignified appearance which characterises the Trongate or Argyle Street of Glasgow.* The **TRADES HALL** (now demolished) was designed by the Town's architect Samuel Bell in 1776, and stood much further into the Market Place than its replacement. The erection of this oddly elegant building on the site of the former shambles was a sign of the growing prosperity of Dundee tradesmen. Prior to this they had met in the open, in the town's burial ground, which as a result, became christened the Howff (meeting place). The hall was not dissimilar to many contemporary public buildings elsewhere in Britain: a classical ideal pavilion, translated by rustic hands into something different. The dumpy tower or cupola arising above the pediment was a solecism borrowed from William Adam's Town House, but in form reflected the tastes of a still earlier generation. The ground floor was rusticated, with canted shop windows, with a pleasantly proportioned first floor, all in Ionic columns. The west end of Market Square was closed by the now demolished **UNION HALL** (originally English Chapel), designed by Samuel Bell in 1783. Although less imposing than the Trades Hall, the simple device of a pedimented, gabled, facade with a gigantic Venetian window served very well. Both buildings were removed as a consequence of William Mackison's radical Improvement Act of 1871 which widened the Seagate, the Murraygate, and Commercial Street, pushing the latter north-westward to Albert Square.

above: the 1776 Trades Hall by Samuel Bell. Behind the Hall can be seen the new Clydesdale Bank which still survives (see p. 18): the Seagate leads off to the right, and the old, narrow Murraygate to the left. *below:* **The Executive** — Henry Kay's caricature of the Town Council in the early 19th century.

above: William Adam's Town House (from Vitruvius Scoticus). *below:* a photograph of the building prior to its demolition.

THE TOWN HOUSE was designed by William Adam in 1731. This original design, from *Vitruvius Scoticus,* shows the classical replacement for Dundee's crumbling sixteenth-century Tolbooth, virtually as built. The ground level piazza, the focus for all trysting in Dundee and known as the **PILLARS** was a clever fusion of traditional Scots arcading now surviving only in Edinburgh and Elgin, and the classical theory of dignifying the major rooms by elevating them to first-floor level, enlivened with details taken from the Aberdonian architect James Gibbs. Dundee's Town House — apart from that in Sanquhar, was unique in Scotland: all other communities were using or repairing their semi-fortified sixteenth- and seventeenth-century Netherlandish Tolbooths. By opting for a major building of the new style, Dundee went for bust — and that, in consequence of having to pay for this building, was how the Town Council remained for a number of years to come.

Adam's is an interesting combination of rustic baroque, Scottish detail, and classical motifs, giving a dumpy appearance. Its glories internally were the set of rooms on the first floor, and a fine oval staircase. A hopelessly insecure gaol existed in the attics, soon to be replaced by others first in the cellars, and then in an extension. The site chosen for the Town House was much criticised in later years as lacking in dignity, and the soft stone which had been used crumbled rapidly. The building was then recased in cement, requiring frequent repainting.

During Dundee's rapid nineteenth-century expansion, the combination of the inconspicuous site and poor surface condition led frequent commentators to suggest that the Town House was no longer worthy of the City. James Caird, one of the city's industrial barons, offered to donate a new City Hall and Concert Hall, just before the First World War. It seems clear that in making this donation, he anticipated the demolition of the Town House so as to enhance the setting of his 2 munificence. The **CAIRD HALL** was designed by James Thomson 1914-22, at the back of an elevated platform, and contains an opulent concert hall executed by Scott Morton. It was in this hall that Sir Thomas Beecham invited Dundonians, should they dislike his performance, to throw marmalade at him always provided, he requested, they removed it from the jar first. The quality of the building is clear, enhanced to some extent by the gift of the massive colonnade from Caird's sister Mrs Marryat, reputedly to compensate for the loss of the Pillars. Nonetheless, City Square itself remains frigid, impersonal, forbidding: everything the *Pillars* was not. Here is an opportunity for imaginative redesign, — perhaps even the relocation of the Wishart Arch (see p. 33) once it is marooned by the Inner Ring Road. The **CITY CHAMBERS,** on the west, was designed in 1924 by Sir John J. Burnet, Scotland's finest architect, as a substitute for Thomson's even more frigid scheme of the same year, and built in 1930-31. Unfortunately, James MacLellan Brown, the City Engineer's architect, tampered with the Square facade to match his equally tedious commercial wing across the square: leaving only the polished, Crichton Street posterior of the Chambers, as a monument to Burnet.

3 **CRICHTON STREET.** In 1779 the council purchased Dr Crichton's large house "for a New Street to go down to the Shore for the more conveniency of the publick" thus creating Dundee's first non-medieval route from the High Street to the sea, too narrow to be really effective. The east side is entirely occupied by the Burnet City Chambers. The west side retains an attractive mix of buildings, slightly curving on its slope, including no. **11-13** a maverick building in brilliantly coloured brickwork with oriels by the Glaswegian architect W. J. Anderson; and the sleek **ROYAL INSURANCE COMPANY** building at the foot by James Parr and Partners, 1971 in dark glass and gleaming metal.

28 HIGH STREET, built about 1785, is a plain four storey building with quoined angles and a wallhead gable facing the street: representative of the standard douce burgh architecture which abounded in Dundee's central streets in the late eighteenth century.

THE OVERGATE CENTRE, designed by Ian Burke, Hugh Martin and Partners in 1963 commemorates the Overgait (formerly Argylisgait) the main western route out of ancient Dundee, and the traditional site of a Royal Mint, and the birthplace of the Scots historian Hector Boece. The post war replanning of central Dundee led to the annihilation of the Overgait, and the construction of the shopping centre. A development of this type has to be seen in the context of its time.

The historian, Dr A. H. Millar, visited Caird a few days before his death to suggest that the retention of the old Town House would enhance the new, and claimed to have converted him; but the latter died before communicating any such conversion. The Town House was duly demolished — as a contribution to the alleviation of unemployment, in 1931. Millar's subsequent plea to the Historical Association of Scotland is one which people have repeated since, in their attempts to retain for Dundee a sense of genius loci: *the despicable philistinism which masquerades under the name of modern utility has lately run riot in Dundee, as in other Scots burghs, and has reached a stage when firm protests must be raised against reckless demolition.*

above: The Caird Hall. *below:* Crichton Street in 1900.

McKean

Dundee District Libraries

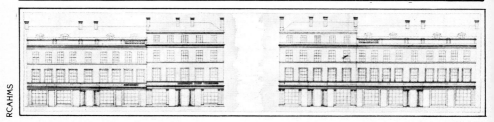

top: Reform Street, original elevation.
above: 34 Reform Street: what William Burn did to George Angus' original pavilion block seen just left of centre in the top drawing. *below:* As it is now.

[4] **REFORM STREET.** George Angus 1832. This was the first major road laid out as a result of William Burn's improvement proposals of 1824-25 which, by cutting through another hill, opened the town to the north. It is the finest neo-classical street to survive in Dundee, the vista at the top being well closed by the splendid seminaries, or High School (see p. 47). It is one of the few to achieve the combination of adequate breadth, adequate length, and adequate coherence of design comparable, in its way, to streets in Aberdeen, Edinburgh and Glasgow. The design is regency in flavour and, unlike comparable streets elsewhere, it was always designed for shops. Those were to be uniformly pilastered and balustrated, with Greek Ionic doorpieces to the business chambers and flats above.

Reform Street contains a number of later, individual structures of some interest. **MEADOW HOUSE,** 1867 by James Maclaren was formerly Lamb's Temperance Hotel, and is now the headquarters of the Alliance Trust. Lamb was a notoriously idiosyncratic citizen whose son collected the vast archive of drawings, sketches and other memorabilia, now in the City Library. His elephantine book *Old Dundee* virtually bankrupted the family but preserved the architectural history of Dundee for posterity. Meadow House was constructed as an architectural riposte to the National Bank across the street, and was refitted by Thoms and Wilkie. The **ROYAL BANK,** 1863, by the Town's architect William Scott, was the building Meadow House was trying to upstage. It is a romanised version of the original George Angus designs, with Roman doric pilasters, and a *piano nobile* enriched with consoles and pediments. **34 REFORM STREET,** 1840, was by William Burn, who ignored the original Angus design for the site and produced a somewhat taller Italian renaissance palace, later remodelled and extended *a posteriori* by George Shaw Aitken in 1880. **BANK STREET,** opening to the left, is principally notable (now that

Kinnaird Hall, through whose high arched roof a suffragette was lowered to embarass Winston Churchill, is demolished) for nos. **7-9,** designed piecemeal by the Owers as sumptuous offices for Sir John Leng, the most outstanding of the Dundee Advertiser's editors.

above: Reform Street. *below:* Bank Street before alteration.

RCAHMS

above: Clydesdale Bank: original drawing showing the carvings, urns and other details now removed. *top right:* As it is now. *below:* Gardyne's House.

McKean: from Lamb's Old Dundee

Wishart

GARDYNE'S HOUSE, Grays Close, 70-73 High Street, 1600, rebuilt internally earlier nineteenth century. The only survivor of the 4th burgh of Scotland of the sixteenth century, lies hidden up a close behind a plain, rendered, eighteenth-century tenement. As the major Royal Burgh in this part of Scotland, Dundee attracted to it the town houses of the greater and lesser nobility, gentry and clergy of Angus, north Fife, and east Perthshire.

Gardyne's house illustrates how Dundee held its own, in terms of quality, with the other great burghs; for it is a five-storey L-shaped block, subsequently much altered. Internal rebuilding revealed tempera ceilings with poems and mottos; and the rugged exterior of large hewn stones is an echo of all the others now surviving only in Lamb's *Old Dundee.*

5**CLYDESDALE BANK,** 94-6 High Street. William Spence 1876. Underscaled triangular block which fails to enclose the east end of the Market Place as did its predecessor, the Trades Hall. Of course, the City authorities wanted to ease the congestion in Murraygate and Seagate caused by the Hall, and used its demolition to widen both, thus giving Spence a much reduced site. Despite its giant Corinthian order and richly sculptured Renaissance details, the bank really requires another storey to give it presence.

6**LOWER COMMERCIAL STREET.** The Seagate north corner was designed by Alexander Johnston 1877, who also designed the entire stretch between Murraygate and Seagate. The two bottom storeys of the corner building are constructed of iron. This street, along with Whitehall Street and Crescent, were the largest undertakings of the 1871 Improvement Act, driven through the heart of the old town *leaving wide streets, open spaces and stately buildings.*

Pressure was applied to ensure that the elevations followed the lead of Mackison the City Engineer. Maclaren and Aitken, who designed the rather French **CALCUTTA BUILDINGS** in 1877 fought back, with some success. John Bruce's 1887 Seagate corner is more lickspittle.

left: St Paul's Cathedral: original proposal by G. G. Scott. *below:* As it is now.

Dundee District Libraries

Stanley Turner

7**ST PAUL'S EPISCOPAL CATHEDRAL CHURCH,** Castle Hill. Sir George Gilbert Scott, 1853. An episcopal stronghold clutched to the side of Dundee's ancient castle rock, this superb Gothic revival church was built for the reforming Bishop Alexander Penrose Forbes. Hemmed in on most sides, the church soars skywards in a way that won support from the very beginning. The *Building Chronicle,* in 1854, considered that: *The new Episcopal Church on the Castle Hill seems destined to form a striking instance of the prejudice a fine building may suffer from an ill-chosen site. It is hemmed in on the west by tall buildings, with scarcely a footpath around it, while all around the other sides a glimpse can only be got of its elaborate features through rifts between old houses.* **The Ecclesiologist,** the

19

above: Castle Chambers. *below right:* Royal Bank — original drawing.

UK Journal of the devotees of the Oxford Movement, and the sole arbiters of architectural propriety in the Gothic Revival differed. The Church, it said *gains much by its unequalled site — a steep rock springing up in the midst of the old quarter of a populous town. The skill of its designer is, however, shown in his having made the most of this opportunity. The treatment is purely Northern and Teutonic, like the plan of the building itself. In it, everything fits into its own place and is in harmony with the remaining structure. The really excellent glass by Mr Hardman which fills all the windows of the apse, is a great additional embellishment. St Paul's stands high among the Churches of the Revival. All concerned in the undertaking have to congratulate themselves on a rare success. In the nave everything is sacrificed to height, and the effect is worth the sacrifice . . . we most heartily congratulate Mr Scott on this very successful work.* In short, one of the finest examples of the high-flown and aristocratic Gothic revival was to be found surrounded by factory chimneys in that distant Scottish City few had, until then, deemed worth visiting. The reredos, with mosaics, is by Salviati of Venice; the spire is 210 ft high; and the surrounding steps and walls have a certain grandeur. **CASTLE HILL HOUSE,** 1 High Street (but within the Cathedral complex) is a late eighteenth century three-storey

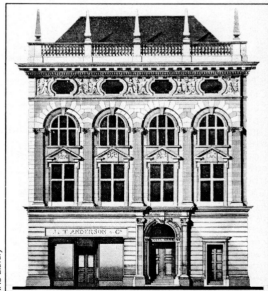

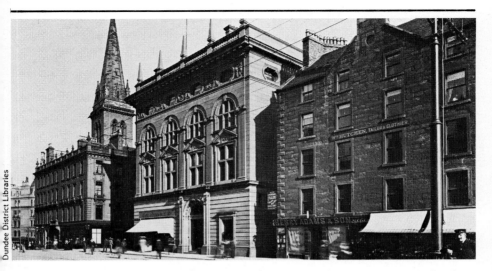

merchant's house in provincial Georgian style: rubble built with dressed quoins, with generally late eighteenth century details, a bow facing south, and a later, two-storey porch.

ROYAL BANK, 3-4 High Street. Sir George Washington Browne 1899. On the corner of Castle Street, the Bank has enormous, classical presence, of a quality not known in Dundee during the real classical period. Originally, the off-centre entrance was balanced by a shop front to the left. The building has a high glass domed banking hall, recently lavishly modernised with costly marbles; and its two facades are dominated by the enormous semi-circular stone bays rising through two storeys, topped by a pinnacled balustrade.

8**CASTLE STREET** from 1795. This "elegant street with several fine buildings" as a visitor described it in 1842, was the first major road between the High Street and the Sea. It was "literally scooped out of a huge rock by force of gunpowder", the rock being the basaltic Black Rock on which Dundee's castle used to stand. Dundee's crucial position on the main northern coastal route and its importance as a defensible base for sea-borne supplies earned it more sieges and sackings than any comparable Scots town. The first castle was damaged by William Wallace, repaired by Edward 1st, finally to be obliterated by Robert the Bruce. There are no subsequent records, and the earliest illustrations of the rock indicate only a hill projecting into the sea,

above: High Street showing the Royal Bank with St Paul's spire behind.

Sir John Stewart, *"A Lloyd George Whisky Baronet . . . a bootlegging pal of Mr Lloyd George"* according to his creditors, had purchased his baronetcy from Maundy Gregory for £50,000, which was refunded from the Lloyd George fund when bankruptcy threatened.

below: Sir John Stewart's offices at 40 Castle Street.

Davies

21

above: The Royal Arch (now demolished) erected to commemorate the visit of Queen Victoria. *below:* Exchange Coffee House and Castle Street behind.

capped by a statue flanked by an old Inn which a lying but persistant legend identified with the medieval castle's magazine, and the Town's Mill to the east.

Castle Street used to be striking for its view: leading fairly steeply down hill to the Docks. Much of its panache has been forfeited now it stutters downhill into the Tay Bridge approach roads. Most of the surviving buildings date from the early nineteenth century, such as **CASTLE CHAMBERS,** no. 26, which has a fine doorway and pillared ground floor. Nos. 7-21 retain, above shop fascia level, the dignified, pedimented facade of Samuel Bell's former **THEATRE ROYAL** (1809) still with its bust of Shakespeare in the roundel in the pediment. **No. 40** is a slender, sumptuous, polished granite and bronze facade of 1919 by Frank Thomson, designed for the whisky magnate Sir John Stewart, who committed suicide in 1924. Thomson's first proposal was rejected with the instruction that he had to return by lunchtime with a better one if he wished to retain the commission. The interior is particularly lavish, with a barrel vault over the staircase. The corner block with Exchange Street is a handsome, plainly elegant design with Greek Doric columns by David Mackenzie, 1832, one of three brothers, all of whom were architects.

[9]**EXCHANGE COFFEE HOUSE,** (now Winter's) 15 Shore Terrace, by George Smith, 1828. A grand monument to Dundee's mercantile marine pre-eminence, by the distinguished architect later responsible for Lynedoch and Woodside Crescents in Glasgow's West End.

As in the town house, the grand rooms were on the first floor, the fact clearly identified by the elegant Ionic order, sitting above the more squat Doric base of the ground floor. The building was a Coffee House, Assembly Rooms, Merchant's Library and Reading Room. Most of the building survives well, with its fine staircase at the rear, and coved ceiling in the main hall.

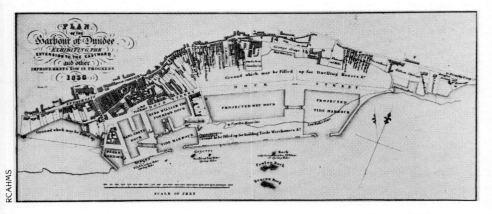

THE SHORE, HARBOUR AND DOCKS

Dundee Harbour Works in 1836.

Dundee owed its original prosperity to its Market Town and Royal Burgh status, due, almost entirely, to its sea-trade: partially ferry traffic from north Fife, but principally commercial trading with Northern Europe. The sixteenth-century Wedderburns had a member of the family constantly in residence at Elsinore, so necessary was it to oversee Danish customs clearance. By mid seventeenth century its harbour must have been substantial by virtue of the 60 ships recorded as having been plundered by Monk; although not sufficiently well built to withstand the storm of 1658. One may guess that the promontory of St Nicholas Craig had simply acted as a breakwater. Daniel Defoe, writing in 1723 noted the linen trade with England, the Norway trade, the east country trade to Danzig, Koenigsberg and Riga, with imports of iron, tar, copper, pitch and deals from Sweden. *These several trades* wrote Defoe, *occasion a concourse of shipping at the port; and there are not a few ships belonging to the place. It has but an indifferent harbour, but the Tay is a large, safe and good road. . . .* In 1772 Thomas Pennant noted the difficulties caused by shifting sand bars, and it was not

In the late eighteenth century Dundee had no route to the sea in which two carriages or carts could pass. The Council was then under the firm dictatorial thumb of Provost Alexander Riddoch who, until his deposition by Parliament in 1819 appeared to run the city single handedly. It was the far sighted public spirit of the man that he anticipated the necessity for new streets — Crichton, Castle, and Tay. In canny style, however, he ensured that prior to the opening of those streets he was the owner of the land to be expropriated: an early example of Tamany Hall politics in the City. The Provost also reserved the best frontages to his own use. Furthermore, although the new streets were wider than existing communications between the town and sea, the streets were far narrower and more poorly laid out than were contemporary developments in Glasgow and Edinburgh.

Thomas Telford, who was called in by the Town in 1814 wrote later (in terms of such rectitude that one must imagine what really lay behind them) that: *the harbour-dues were entirely in the hands of the corporation, collected and applied promiscuously with the town revenue; and in the ten years previous to 1815, although £13,817 had been collected, no more than £1,183 had been expended upon the harbour and wharves. But it was now discovered that the prosperity of the port was connected with that of the district at large. . . . From the past conduct of the corporation, and their confined views, no prospect existed of obtaining suitable accommodation under their management as indeed was fully evidenced by their instructions to me. . . . A number of public spirited individuals having interposed, overpowered the corporation, and the exclusive management of the harbour was put into the hands of public commissioners. . . . The management of the port was taken out of (their) hands because their views did not keep pace with the growing demands of commerce.*

until the early nineteenth century, and the political upheaval in the burgh, that adequate steps were taken.

Defoe had also noted that Dundee was not a sea-side town as such: *The town of Dundee stands at a little distance from the Tay, but they are joined by a causeway or walk, well pav'd with flat freestone, and rows of trees are planted on either side of the walk, which makes it very agreeable.*

During the eighteenth century, that walk became obliterated by warehouses and the like: and Yeaman Shore became built-up, its villas having garden walls to the sea's edge.

Eastwards, the shore curved inland from the castle rock, following the backs of houses, warehouses and ship building premises along Seagait. The current shore line derives mainly from the efforts of the great Victorian dock builders: and the arrival of the Arbroath and Dundee railway, which drove a causeway through the sea, roughly along the line of Camperdown Street, leaving a large inland pool to the north between it and Seagait.

The business of the Docks might be said to be the first trump in the action leading to the final defeat of the faction led by Provost Alexander Riddoch. In two points relating to the Docks, the Town's administration had been scarcely efficient. Since 1803 the tonnage at the Docks had increased by over 10%; yet the City spent no money on its harbour or wharves, then still entirely tidal. The same nonchalant attitude was taken to the Ferry to Fife, as noted in 1845: *"the Ferry was so badly managed it might have been said to be no Ferry at all — the boatman being almost constantly the judges of the times of sailing as well as the regulators of the amount of fare. . . . Extortion and incivility produced their certain result — almost total ruin to the concern.*

Earl Grey Dock in the late 19th century. Note the arrival not only of the steam tug and sand boat, but the spire of St Pauls, and the factory chimneys. The Green market lay just beyond the left edge of the photograph.

Stanley Turner Collection

Telford was appointed to produce *an extensive floating dock* and *graving dock for large vessels,* sufficiently far advanced for Robert Southey, Poet Laureate — who accompanied Telford on one of his round-Scotland site visits — to record it as *a huge floating dock and the finest graving dock I ever saw.* It was completed by 1825 and, by 1826, the tonnage levels of 1813 had more than doubled. In 1831 Telford was consulted about converting the eastern tidal dock into an enclosed harbour, for which he proposed the novelty of 55' wide lockgates made of cast iron. The works were supervised by the appointed harbour engineer James Leslie (one of the two designers of the Customs House) and completed in 1834, being named the Earl Grey Dock.

The Shore below the Vault was the location for Dundee's celebrated Greenmarket and adjacent fish market west of the Castle Rock and it contained a number of ancient streets and houses. W. J. Smith, writing in 1873 described the scene thus: *This quarter of the town is greatly frequented on Saturday evenings, the attractions being of an extremely varied and diverse character. In close juxtaposition may be seen the street preacher addressing the crowd, the quack doctor vending his nostrums, the cheap John and the ballad-singer, galvanic batteries, beef and sweetie stands, and exhibitions of dead and living wonders, forming altogether a curious medley.*

McKean

Dundee University

In 1844 Captain Washington remembered how *within the living memory of man, the harbour was a crooked wall enclosing but a few smuggling or fishing craft, compared to which the alterations and improvements to Dundee's sea-face almost exceed belief, having every requisite for a first-class commercial port.* It is difficult now to comprehend the extent of the pre-eminence of Dundee's port in the nineteenth century. Its expansion was linked to the Jute trade from India, and the South Atlantic whaling trade. It is sobering to recall that by 1870, 216 ships and 18 whalers were registered at Dundee docks, trading with the then entire known world, a fact recorded even on sea shanties:

Oh the noble fleet of Whalers out sailing from
 Dundee,
Well manned by British sailors to work them on the
 sea;
On the western ocean passage none with them can
 compare,
For there's not a ship could make the trip as the
 Balaena, I declare.

By 1912 the harbour occupied 190 acres all on land reclaimed from the river, totalling 3.5 miles of quayside, serviced by 10 miles of railway, handling over 800,000 tonnes of trade.

top: The view to St Paul's Cathedral from the Victoria Dock: the stern of the Unicorn on the left. *above:* The whaler Balaena. *below:* Dundee Custom House and Harbour Chambers.

14 The grand **CUSTOM HOUSE AND HARBOUR CHAMBERS,** designed by James Leslie and John Taylor in 1842-3 is a symbol of what has been lost. It is one of the largest

Walker

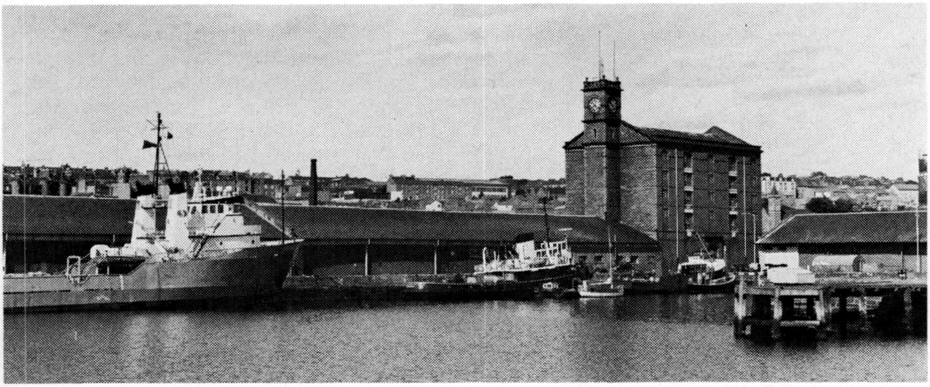

McKean

Customs Houses in Scotland, three storeys tall, thirteen bays long and dominated by a massively projecting centre, capped by a pediment supported by four huge Ionic columns, themselves standing upon an arched, rusticated ground floor.

10 The only surviving Docks are the **CAMPERDOWN** (Charles Ower Senior 1863-5), the **VICTORIA,** the Graving Docks and a tidal fish dock. One must be grateful for the survival of any water near central Dundee, and the docks have the nostalgic atmosphere of a Sleeping Beauty waiting to be kissed back to life. Victoria retains a stone shed with curved corners, probably an early workshop; and the tall, six-storey Italianate grain elevator, with clock tower. Its finest possession, however, amidst naval and north sea oil vessels is the frigate **UNICORN,** a lone survivor of "Britain's wooden walls", dating from 1824. This fine vessel had 46 guns and, for many years, served as a training ship.

It is currently being restored by voluntary effort.

The scanty remains of Dundee's fine seaface offer other relics. To the west, the road now occupies the *Esplanade* recovered from the sea in the early 1870's, previous to which the railway was at the shore's edge. The fine towered baronial Caledonian railway station has gone, although the earlier station survives with the uncompromisingly box-shaped but oddly elegant post war ticket hall. Yeaman Shore has been engulfed by the Inner Ring Road, leaving as the main west landmark the
1 recently cleaned **TAY HOTEL.** Designed in 1898 by Robert Hunter, the building clearly owes significant architectural patronage to Mackison's adjacent Whitehall Crescent.

above: The Victoria dock looking north east toward the granary. *below:* The frigate Unicorn and its sectional drawing.

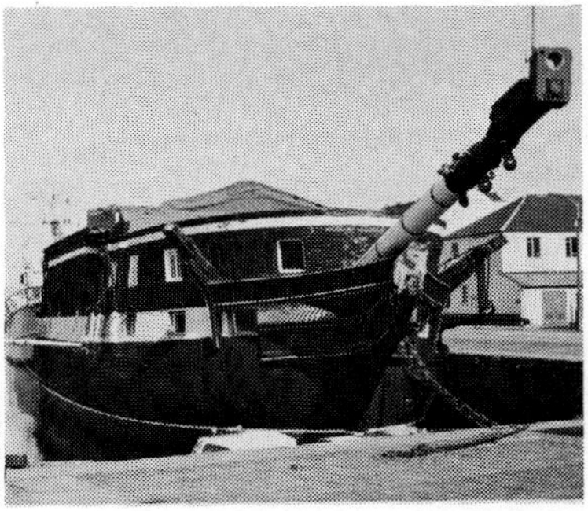

McKean

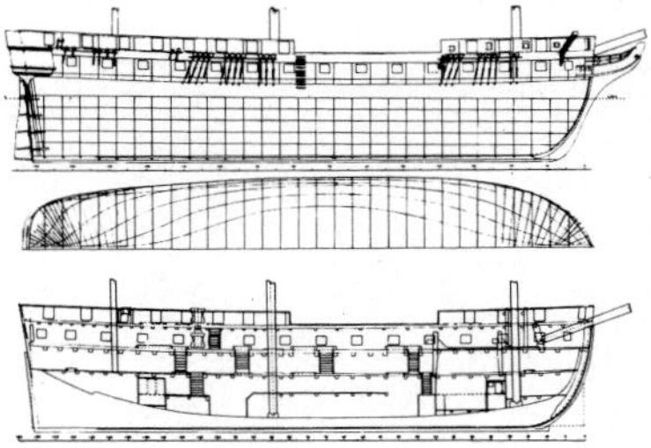

above: The Tay Hotel. *below:* Leisure centre. *bottom:* Tayside House.

New arrivals at the western end are the [12]**LEISURE CENTRE,** by James Parr and Partners 1974; although failing to exploit its riverside location, it is a good building of its type being enclosed, square, low lying in an oasis of motorway and trees providing the twentieth-century version of the Roman bread and circuses, planned to be the first phase of a [13]much larger Coliseum. **TAYSIDE HOUSE,** also by James Parr and Partners 1976, is a tall, elegant block of offices. One might well question whether either the Tay Bridge or this block should have penetrated so far into the navel of Dundee. Given that it has, accepting that a Regional Headquarters is basically an administrative building, and noting that site restrictions compelled a narrow building, Tayside House does rather well in an international sort of way.

The remainder of the Shore is difficult to appreciate: much is difficult to reach. Note, however, some plain buildings by the Exchange Coffee House; the block between Gellatly Street and Candle Lane, opposite the Customs House, displaying a good assembly of styles from Queen Anne to 1880 Germanic horror — gothic of the Watson Fothergill (of Nottingham) type: culminating in the domed Sailor's Home by David Maclaren 1881. Of particular note is **20 DOCK STREET,** 1891 by James Maclaren, the headquarters of the Dundee Perth and London Shipping Company and once also the home base of the Falklands Islands Company. It is an elegant stone, Renaissance detailed block with cast iron mullions.

SEAGATE

The heart of Old Dundee, formerly location of Tolbooth and Cross, closed by the East Port to the east, and bounded by maritime activities on the south. It was the principal street of the medieval town, in which many of the notable families of the county had their town houses. *It is said,* wrote an anonymous commentator in 1799, *that the Cowgate and Seagate met with great desolation when the town was stormed by Montrose . . . and also at Monk's storming in 1651 — from which it has never fully recovered. When I first came to the town in 1756, there were very few inhabitants in this street; some old homes near the East End, with several homes in ruins, but chiefly yards . . . the only tolerable dwelling homes were Provost Robertson's on the north side . . . and some old homes opposite.* The City inexorably moved west, and in the later eighteenth century with the expansion of the docks eastward, the Seagate and associated areas became more of an industrial backland. By 1845, *a few excellent homes had been built but there is great room for improvement.* It is now a traffic route with some isolated monuments, particularly: **SEAGATE NO. 2 WAREHOUSE,** designed by Christopher J. Bisset in 1868. It is a fine Bonded Warehouse, in ashlar with plain front facing the street, topped by wheatsheaf chimneys, with an elegant facade down Candle Lane. The **LOYAL ORDER OF ANCIENT SHEPHERDS,** 97 Seagate, by David Baxter (of Johnston and Baxter), 1907, is a blushingly scrubbed, Edwardian red and white patterned building of vaguely Jacobean details; now in multiple use: well worth comparing to Baxter's earlier *performance opposite, the 1897* **ROBERTSON'S BOND,** unfortunately still begrimed: a younger and altogether more strident piece of turretted Jacobean. The **SCWS BUILDING,** on the corner of Queen Street, a 1934 corner building in Stylish American Art Deco: whose sleek stone frame encloses orange painted metal curtain-walling, was designed by Charles Armour. It must have been quite the fancy thing of the time. Just to the east, lies **ST ROQUE'S LIBRARY,** Blackscroft, by James Thomson 1910. Blackscroft is just outside the eastern boundary of old Dundee, in Wallace-Craigie. St Roque's later became corrupted to *Semirookie.* The Library, now a club, is a single storey, French Renaissance pavilion, in a formal triangular garden on a fine site overlooking the Tay. The design may have been the work of a gifted London draughtsman, William Careless.

Baxter Clark Paul

above: The Seagate, St Paul's spire and Robertson's Bond.

below: St Roque's library (original drawing).

Dundee District Council

DUNDEE AND THE MILLS

17 THE LOWER DENS WORKS, 2 Princes Street, St Roque's Lane. Peter Carmichael (of Baxter Brothers) and Randolph Elliot, 1850. Dundee has no finer Victorian symbol than the Dens Mills. Located at this point to use the water power of the now culverted Dens Burn, these works comprised the headquarters of the Baxter Brothers, an Angus family who settled in Dundee in the early nineteenth century, and became synonymous with major benefactions to the City, such as the Albert Institute (see p. 41), Baxter Park, and University College, Dundee (now the University). Much of Victorian Dundee was controlled by family dynasties, and the rivalry between the Baxters, Grimonds, Coxs' and Gilroys was legendary. The Baxters had the sense, however, to admit an outsider into their partnership — the engineer Peter Carmichael, and it was on his enquiring, innovative genius that the Baxters thrived, and, unusually, kept the Dens Mills on flax and not on jute.

An indication of the Carmichael determination may be seen from the way he spent his annual holiday: *Improvements were constantly being introduced as they were hit upon, heard of, or seen elsewhere. It was then my custom to make an annual excursion in the quest of mechanical improvements.*

top: The Dens complex in its heyday.
above: The Upper Dens Mills.

The **UPPER DENS MILL** (soon to be converted to housing) is the principal survivor of the Baxter Empire. Despite Carmichael's own statement, *If you can see your way to put up substantial buildings they will certainly keep their value. I have always been rather stingy in buildings, preferring to spend on labour-saving machinery*, this Mill, designed with the help of Glaswegian engineer Randolph Elliott, is a fine monument, with a central engine house, and a tower capped by a cast-iron and slate cupola at one end. It is a fireproof building with wide spans and gothic cast-iron roof trusses, all the machinery on each floor powered from the centre.

THE MILLS were complete communities, employing their own schoolmasters to educate the mill boys when not working. At their peak, in 1871, some 5,000 workers were employed by Baxters, 2,000 more than Cox, and one tenth of all those employed in jute, flax, and linen in Scotland. From the records, Baxters do not appear to have been the worst employers. Although anti-union, the paternalistic tradition seems to have ensured reasonable conditions, for the time.

But Dundee's dependence upon the Mill economy was unique in Scotland. It had ancient origins. Hector Boece wrote of his home town of the fifteenth century, *Dundee, the town quhair we were born; quhair many virteous and lauborius pepill are in, making of cloth.* Dundee's singularity in the nineteenth century was that it had become dependent on a single product — jute; and that the majority of jute workers were female. In time, Mill workers created an entire subculture of language, behaviour and initiation rites. There were strict class distinctions amongst them, the top being the weavers: *the weavers, winders and sack machinists are a hard working, thrifty, and self respecting class of workers. They impress visitors by the neatness of their dress and the decorum of their manners. There is nothing of the typical mill girl about them, although she does exist in some parts of Dundee.* (Thus the view of the Dundee Social Union reporting to the British Association in 1912.)

In 1912, of a total working population of 34,414, — 23;369 or well above 60% were women. Of the remainder (ie men) only 23% were over 20, the bulk being boys employed in the mills. Their life style was such that, in 1904, one in every four infants died. The then Medical Officer of Health attributed this to the *exceptional industrial conditions of Dundee, the*

Wishart

above: The Lower Dens Mill.

Oh! dear me, the mull's gaen fest,
Puir wee shifters canna get a rest,
Shiftin' bobbins coarse and fine,
Wha wad work for twa and nine.

The poor wee shifters were children, working half time, and earning half the 5/6d weekly wage of the older children working full time. (Juteopolis: Dr William Walker.)

The Cowgate gusset, once home of the Grimonds.

DUNDEE'S position at the forefront of reform — presaging a perpetual trend or radicalism in the city — was enhanced by the activities of James Wedderburn who, sometime before 1540 *composed in the form of tragedie the beheading of Johne the Baptist, which was acted at the West Port of Dundie, wherin he carped roughlie the abusses and corruptiouns of the Papists. He compiled the Historie of Dionysius . . . wherein he likewise nipped the Papists. . . . This James had a good gift of poesie and made diverse comedeis and tragedeis in the Scottish tongue.* Wedderburn was one of a triumvirate of brothers, James, John and Robert, who produced the celebrated **Gude and Godlie Ballatis** in 1567 *(ane compendious book of Godly and Spirituall songs collected out of sundrie parts of scripture, with sundrie of other Ballates changed out of prophaine songis for avoyding of sinne and harlotrie)* which, according to Trevor Royle, is *an early indication of the combination of coarseness and refinement that was to characterise so many of the best collections of Scottish traditional songs.*

very low wages paid to the unskilled male worker in our mills and factories, and the large number of women (including married women) employed in them.

There are 30 major industrial survivors in Dundee, the majority concentrated where water power was available: 17 to the west around the old Scouring Burn route, and 15 to the east linked to the route of the Dens Burn.

18 **COWGATE**

Another historic street ruined by the Burgh's drift westward, and the early, uncontrolled arrival of tanneries, breweries and Mills on all sides, from which it developed into the market and headquarters of the linen industry certainly until 1882. For a long time, it was the custom of Dundee's merchants to meet — to use as the Rialto — in St Andrew's Square, at the head of the Cowgate where King Street now debouches. The late Georgian, bow-fronted gusset with King Street became the head office and, for some time, the home of the Grimonds, under whose control Edward and Robertson added the heavy classical embellishments in 1877. The singularities of a tight triangular site means that the pleasant, shallow bay-fronted Georgian houses alongside, form the de-facto rear of early nineteenth-century classical homes in King Street. At this stage it is impossible to tell whether they were added *a posteriori.*
Although the restoration of the western end of the Cowgate would be an exciting challenge and a townscape necessity, the centre of the throughfare is soon to receive an Inner Ring Road leaving, unless rescued, the Cowgate's most historic relic marooned on the far shore. That relic is the old City gateway, the **WISHART ARCH** which may predate 1548. The burgh had done little to defend itself after the destruction of the Castle on the Black Rock as witness the 1556 decription of the French invasion of Angus at the behest of Mary of Guise: *The Scots care so little for fortifying themselves that the inhabitants of Dundee have no other place of refuge or fort to which they may retire save their own houses.* It is clear from the Wishart Arch that a defensive gate of this type — with a main carriage arch and a footpath arch — would offer only token resistance to armed invasion. On the other hand it might well perform more effectively as a central point to prevent outsiders from flooding the tightly controlled city with their cut price goods. The gate gained its name

from the Reformer George Wishart, who is
said to have used it as a pulpit from which to
preach to the converted during the plague of
1544. However, both this gate's original
location and its date are uncertain. Certain
only is the fact that its legendary connection
with the Reformer prevented its demolition.

The Wishart Arch.

Wishart

top: 7-19 King Street.

bottom: Wishart Memorial Church.

THE WISHART MEMORIAL
CHURCH ❧ DUNDEE 1899
T MARTIN CAPPON FRIBA
DUNDEE

RIAS Library

19 KING STREET
This *generally well built street* was in 1820 according to Peter Carmichael, *one of the most ornamental parts of the town, with substantial, regular and handsome buildings erected on each side.* It was opened in the late eighteenth century (although not developed until the early nineteenth) to provide an easier route to Forfar and the north east than the precipitous Hilltown route and, unlike the Cowgate, it was provided with a good bridge over the Dens Burn. It was ornamented with several fine churches — the Glasite Kirk, St Andrew's Church, and the Wishart Memorial Church; with the original, classical, Town's Hospital; and with fine late-Georgian terraces on either side. The red stone, former **WISHART MEMORIAL CHURCH** 1901, designed by T. M. Cappon's art-nouveau-inclined assistant W. G. Lamond, traces of whom are most obvious in the wrought iron railings (the rest being in loose, late Gothic) was the church of the missionary Mary Slessor. Beyond the ring road blight is **7-19 KING STREET,** 1815-19 either by, or in the style of David Neave, the then Town's architect: a terrace of good symmetrically designed houses with fanlights, rusticated ground floors, and Doric doorpieces — many sadly painted, disfigured or poorly maintained. **THE GLASITE CHAPEL,** 4 King

Street, was completed in 1777, and is a simple octagon, with a prismatic slate roof, harled walls and stone dressings, for which no architect is known. It stands as the monument to an eighteenth-century Minister, Rev. John Glas, who opted out to form his own sect, now famous for two memories: first, that they married very young; and second, that those attending service were given Kail soup, hence the nickname for the building, the *Kail Kirk*. Recently refurbished by Thoms and Wilkie.

ST ANDREW'S CHURCH, next door, is the surviving masterwork of Samuel Bell. Completed in 1772, it is a grand, simple rectangular church whose design was probably adapted from an original design by James Craig (designer of Edinburgh's New Town). It has fine stone dressings, twin venetian and semi-circular windows, swags, and a splendid west tower, with a steeple which recesses at each higher level in the James Gibbs manner. Thomas Pennant, who saw the church the year it was completed thought that it was *built in a style that does credit to the place, and which shews an enlargement of mind in the presbyterians, who now begin to think that the LORD may be praised in the beauty of holiness.* The contemporary drawing demonstrates the extent to which the church was built in a suburban, if not semi-rural situation. Its construction was a sign of the growing power of the Trades who, only a few years later, commissioned Bell to design their new Hall in the High Street (see p. 13). Peter Carmichael recorded how it looked in the early 1820s: *standing on a rising ground, ornamented with*

top: The Glasite chapel, King Street. *above:* Pennant's 1772 engraving of St Andrew's Church. *left:* St Andrew's Church today.

shrubberies, it had the pretty look of a country church . . . there were seats for the conveners of the Trades and other dignitaries in the front of the church gallery, and there they sat with their gold chains . . . the minister bowed to them at the close of the service and they stood up and returned the bow.

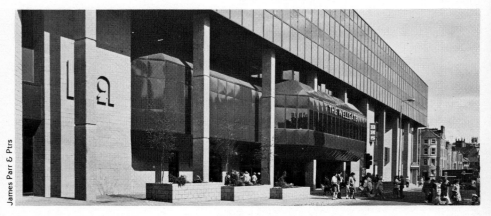

James Parr & Ptrs

The Wellgate Centre, the end of the Cowgate to the right.

20 WELLGATE

Wellgate formed part of the ancient route from the High Street, through Murraygate, up Wellgate to Hilltown and Strathmartine. Once in Wellgate, the incline became severe — so much so that the head of the street ended in the famous Wellgate Steps, an echo of which survives at the northern entrance to the new shopping centre and library by James Parr and Partners, 1977. It is an enclosed centre, on three levels, clad in brown blockwork, and protruding brown fascia. The traders combined with the Council to resurrect a fine old lamp standard above the steps to Victoria Road. Architecturally, Wellgate is of the standard required by international commerce, with a striking, Piranesi-like circular vault to the car park entrance.

THE WATER WAR

The Wellgate earned its name from the Lady Well, at its head, one of the three main sources of water into Dundee until the mid nineteenth century. It had once been famous for its pure water. Yet an 1868 Water Commission on Water Supply found the water to be *piquant to the palate . . . our analysis shows that this is nothing but a very purified sewage to the properties of decomposition of which it owes its pleasant flavour.* It was, reported the Water Commission manager horribly polluted by sewage and by animal matters of the most disgusting origin. The consequences were that Dundee remained an unhealthy city long after others had remedied the matter. Witness the Chief Sanitary Inspector: *the most loathsome of infectious diseases were more or less constantly present in epidemic form. From the year 1860 onwards smallpox, typhus, typhoid and gastric fevers were serious menaces to the health of the community. For many years, there were never less than from 300 to 500 cases.*

The matter of a fresh water supply to the City was known as the *Water War* beginning in 1832 and ranged over decades, with the two factions trying to control the Council. The one faction believed that a rate should be raised to lay on a full supply: the other that water was a commercial operation. The Guildry and the Nine Trades took the latter view: *They did not see the peculiar circumstances that should make men idiots enough to prefer paying by taxation what ought to be vendible in the market like any other commodity.*

Between 1833 and 1837 three separate schemes had been proposed, and blocked, adding £32,000 to the Town's debts with nothing to show for it, hastening the entire burgh toward bankruptcy. According to William Norrie *never was there a dispute conducted with more heat and acerbity as the Water War. Persons who had been the dearest friends for years turned into the most rancorous foes; fathers quarrelled with sons, and brothers with brothers.* Not until 1874 was the principal water supply from Lintrathen established.

Opposite the Wellgate is the former **KING'S THEATRE** (now County Bingo) designed from his London digs by Frank Thomson. A red sandstone building that could well do with a wash, it was celebrated for the fact that Thomson, then an assistant at Niven & Wigglesworth and designing the building from his London digs, was provided with an inaccurate survey by his brother. The difference became evident upon construction for the pit entrance was left high and dry; whereupon the architect sought help from the City Engineer (his father) who obligingly proposed new public lavatories under the road at this point, necessitating raising the road level which fortunately managed to coincide with the requirements of the new building.

The last, dying letter of a local poet called William Knight, written from the Infirmary in 1866, described the course of such a plague: *I was in comfortable lodgings, but the fever broke over Dundee like an avalanche. . . . My lodging-house folks were attacked almost simultaneously. My landlady was carried to the Royal Infirmary: next, her eldest boy. Next, the landlord himself was siezed. . . . I took in a "closer" lad who couldn't get lodgings: poor fellow, he was siezed with the fever and died a day or two after . . . but now my turn came . . . I had not pain and was getting as much as 12 oz of unreduced whisky every 24 hour, so that I was always half-seas over.*

above: The Bank of Scotland, Murraygate.

Wishart

IT WAS in Murraygate that transpired the comedy of the arrest of two American medical students as French spies in 1801. They had been recommended by a fellow Ferry traveller to go to Cooper's Tavern in Murraygate where their odd dress and the blue spectacles of John Bristed, earned them a refusal. They proceeded to talk the innkeeper down in Latin; who admitted them, blocked them in an upper room and called the magistrates. After considerable commotion, during which the Captain of the Militia at Dudhope proposed that *on account of the terror and alarm which these two ragged tatter demalions have thrown all the valourous inhabitants of Dundee, somewhat more than twenty-five-thousand people, you could not punish them more effectively than making them militia men in my company,* they were rescued by being identified by a fellow medical student of Magdalen Yard, and escaped unscathed.

right: the original drawing, without the balustrade mentioned in the contemporary account.

21 MURRAYGATE

The part-pedestrianisation of what, for a long time now, has been Dundee's principal commercial street, provides a rare relief in this traffic dominated city. The retention of the cobbles, tramlines and splendid central, ornamental lampstandards, provides memories of a more confident past. Murraygate used to have two parts: the Narrows (alongside the Trades Hall), and the Broad, a distinction eliminated by the 1871 gouging of Commercial Street. Some pre-1871 buildings survive in the eastern stretch, to remind us how, in Murraygate *the greater part of business of Dundee with foreign parts is transacted. The homes are of moderate height and, in general, regular and well built.* Back in 1745, according to a chronicler, *the landed gentry who (like the woodcocks) did the honour to pass the winter among us strutted about in tiptoe and in sullen hauteur.* The same chronicler notes that by 1799: *The county squires here, for the present, quitted the town. Like Cincinnatus, they have returned to the ploughshares and to their Seats, and have thus become Burgh Seceders.* When you look at what had become of the fashionable part of Dundee — Cowgate, Seagate, Murraygate, you can see why. In planning jargon, there was a failure of zoning: in ordinary English, the city had failed to prevent this area and its backlands from being overrun by breweries, tanneries and mills — all with their particularly neighbourlike effulgences.

A number of interesting buildings survive,

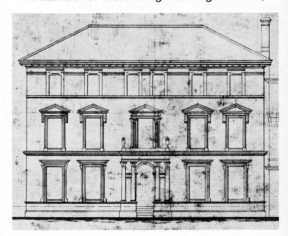

the variety of which, along with their scale, combines to render Murraygate the most engaging single street in the city centre. Note particularly **WOOLWORTHS** 1937, which is typical of the glazed fin style, with cinema entertainment connotations, which was the corporate UK style of the store at the time. **MEADOW ENTRY,** probably by the mason David Rait, 1783, is a simple tenement, with wallhead gable above an arched pend, in need of restoring owner, a relic of the days when this street was the northern end of the town. In the eighteenth century it was a *small narrow close below Quaker Lighton's long tithed land, and called the Meadow's-entry; and there was no other entry from the town to the Meadows but it and James Mathew's Close in the Murraygate.* The north side of Murraygate protected the town from a swamp to the north: *the meadows or greens were then unenclosed, wet and dirty and the health of the inhabitants was much infected from stagnant pools there.* **BANK OF SCOTLAND** 35-39 Murraygate, by David Cousin, 1868, is a fine — possibly the finest in Dundee, — classical palazzo, built for the British Linen Bank (whose architect Cousin was). The history of the Bank is unclear. This July 1854 extract from the **Building Chronicle** indicates that, like so many other buildings in Murraygate, what we see is a graft onto an older building: *The British Linen Bank premises in Murraygate are being enlarged and improved by the erection of a new telling room in the rear, and the extension of the front building. The present telling room is to form the lobby: rather a large one as one may be supposed, and we should think insufficiently lighted. The front is to be re-modelled by the insertion of string course, and crowned by a ponderous cornice and balustrade.* The new telling room at the rear is a very grand hall with a rotunda supported on Corinthian columns.
30 MURRAYGATE includes a fragment of the magnificent 1913 **La Scala** cinema, designed by George A. Boswell of Glasgow. Its exotic facade is still festooned with faience, fins, and swags, and formerly there was a tower with a golden globe. **31 MURRAYGATE** has an unusual peeling doorway grafted, in 1877 by Ireland and Maclaren (whose office it was) onto a late Georgian commercial building. **14-16 MURRAYGATE,** by Gauldie and Hardie 1911, was a stimulating Arts and Crafts shoe-shop, extended upwards from a two-storey, very early eighteenth-century building. Note the Art Nouveau details, and the harled bay

RCAHMS

Gauldie Wright

top: La Scala Cinema now shorn of its tower and golden globe. *above:* Potter's Shoe Shop, 14/16 Murraygate.

right: Commercial Street when first built.
below: the junction with Murraygate.

Dundee District Libraries

RCAHMS

The story of William Mackison, the Burgh Engineer so lambasted by *The Builder* certainly shows him to have been capable. He worked as a solicitor, then trained as an architect and engineer with his uncle Francis Mackison in Stirling, becoming Burgh Surveyor and Town's Architect there and, with David Bryce, the first Fellow of the R.I.B.A. in Scotland. When Dundee's engineer, Fulton, quit to go cattle ranching in Texas, Mackison came in as engineer and speedily undermined Scott, the ailing Town's Architect. The Burgh went along with this, thinking that they would be getting their architectural services free from their engineer. Mackison, however, was putting it on the slate, and in 1906 claimed £40,000 for additional work undertaken outside his normal duties. He was suspended, and then dismissed and took the Town to Court; dying before the case could be heard. His family pursued the case to the house of Lords, ruining themselves in the process.

windows of the Patrick Geddes variety of Arts and Crafts then being built in Edinburgh's Lawnmarket. **7-11 MURRAYGATE,** by W. Alexander, 1896, forms part of the rebuilt **NARROWS**; typical of the 1871 Improvement Act architecture in which the City Architect (Alexander) had to follow the Burgh Engineer. Alexander was appointed to this high honour (£40 p.a. + commissions) by virtue of the fact that Pa owned the *Dundee Courier.*
22 **COMMERCIAL STREET** (High Street to Albert Square) designed by William Mackison (Burgh Engineer) in 1871, is City Improvement Act Architecture by the Master with the aid of John Lessels, who was doing similar work in Edinburgh. *The Builder,* in an otherwise complimentary review of Dundee in August 1898 said this: *Another example of an attempt to treat a street as one complete architectural design, if there were really any design in it. It is, however, only so many yards of pattern-book architecture, a mere medley of tawdry ornaments, the sort of thing that might be expected from one of the gentlemen who build rows of £20 houses in the suburbs. We understand the Burgh Engineer is responsible for the design . . . everyone capable of judging architectural design must regret that a man who is probably exceptionally capable (he would hardly be Burgh Engineer of Dundee if he were not) should have committed such an error of judgement as to attempt work for which his training and experience obviously had not fitted him.* A bit harsh, perhaps. The assembly of florid, French Renaissance details has a collective scale and grandeur that reminds one of contemporary Milan: and brings to Dundee a small amount of architectural cohesiveness that its rigidly independent, anti-planning attitude prevented elsewhere.

Wishart

²³ALBERT SQUARE

The **ALBERT INSTITUTE,** Sir George Gilbert
Scott 1865-7.

Memorials to Albert were the rage
throughout Britain, but Dundee was bankrupt
— not least as a result of the Water War. The
Baxters, their friends and dynastic rivals (some
of whom had caused the town bankruptcy in
that war) formed a private company to build
one ready for the arrival of the British
Association in 1867, resulting in the grandest
Albert Memorial outside London.

Scott's design intentions are worth noting:
The style was to be *of the best period of
pointed Architecture, taking pains to give it such
national characteristics as to render it distinctly
Scottish in general feeling.* Perhaps the giant

Jute, Jam and **Journalism** are Dundee's three contributions to British culture; and of the three, only journalism survives in its native habitat with its former vigour. (The purchase by the Okhai Brothers of the Keiller business looks fair set to revive the jam. Their slogan *Okhai the noo!* seems peculiarly Dundonian.) Thomson's is one of the last surviving Dundee dynasties: celebrated as much for their hard professional training, family idiosyncrasies, and benevolent paternalism — taken, sometimes to remarkable degrees, as for their anti-unionism. Whereas other Dundee tycoons extracted their money from the city and mutated to country lairds, the Thomsons remain yet.

The history of the group is interesting. The flagship — *the Courier and Advertiser* — derives from two opposing papers: the radical *Dundee Advertiser,* founded in 1801 to *establish a paper in which the liberal sentiments of the people could be freely expressed,* and the Conservative *Courier,* founded in 1816. The *People's Friend* and the *People's Journal* joined the *Advertiser* stable in the mid nineteenth century. The group is now as much famous for its comics, and characters such as Biffo the Bear, Oor Wullie, Desperate Dan, and Lord Snooty.

crow-step gables, and the rose-window on the great hall on the first floor represent his Scots sops. He later wrote of Glasgow University, *I adopted a style which I may call my own invention having already initiated it at the Albert Institute in Dundee. It is simply a thirteenth- or fourteenth-century secular style, with the addition of certain Scottish features peculiar in that country in the sixteenth century . . . .*

Scott adapted his unbuilt scheme for Hamburg's Rathaus. The central part of the building was designed to Scott's intentions in 1873 by David MacKenzie, and the Eastern galleries in 1887 by the City Architect, William Alexander, of whose efforts *The Builder* wrote: *Mr Alexander is to be congratulated on not having failed to a far greater extent in a difficult task.* It is a superb building, dogged by a difficult site; isolated by heavy traffic; complicated by a spectacular Renaissance-plan horseshow staircase affixed to the Gothic western flank. It has recently been restored by the District Council Architects, revealing a masterpiece of rich polychromy, the stencils in the hall itself rediscovered for the first time since 1877. Paintings include examples by MacTaggart, Orchardson and Sargent. Statues at the exterior include those to George Duncan, Dundee's first Reform MP by Sir John Steell RA, James Carmichael (the engineer father-in-law to Peter) and Robert Burns, who looks contemplatively westward at D. C. Thomson's cultural empire on the south-west side of the square.

Brooding over everything, and terminating

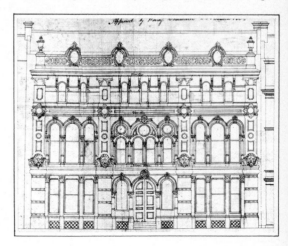

right: The ill-fated Eastern Club, demolished because it would not convert easily into a bank. It was one of the outstanding buildings by the maverick Victorian architect Frederick Pilkington, and stood on the south side of Albert Square.

Dundee District Libraries

left: The Courier building prior to its extension. *below:* Original perspective of the Panmure Street congregational church. *bottom:* Royal Exchange Assurance.

the square to the west, is **THE COURIER BUILDING,** 22 Meadowside, 1902 by Niven and Wigglesworth; the headquarters of D. C. Thomson Ltd. For their new headquarters building, Thomsons chose a firm of London architects, one of whom had local connections, David Barclay Niven being from Angus. Wigglesworth had experience in this field already having travelled to America to visit the William Randolph Hearst empire. The result is a confident, tall, red stone, steel-framed building with engaging sculptural details by Albert Hodge: gigantic columns reach up through several storeys as window dressing for the metal structure behind: and for aficionados of Desperate Dan, may be compared to a good helping of architectural cow pie.

CONGREGATIONAL CHURCH, Panmure Street, by David Bryce, 1855, is a picturesque, demure church with Gothic window, and flanking octagonal towers. The *Building Chronicle* commended the *picturesqueness of disposition and detail, at the same time appeasing economical scruples by introducing nothing that does not perform a structural part in the design.* Adjacent is **ROYAL EXCHANGE ASSURANCE BUILDING** 1957 by Gauldie Hardie Wright and Needham. This plainly elegant, classical 1950's building is well mannered and should be considered good of its time and type, achieving a degree of visual interest within the prevailing climate of puritanism by the central balcony and recessed upper storey.

Richard Davies

43

Original perspective of the Royal Exchange, showing the proposed tower abandoned after foundation failure.

THE ROYAL EXCHANGE, 1854-5, was designed by David Bryce, as Dundee's mercantile centre — to the loss of the Exchange Coffee House down by the shore. Now used by the Chamber of Commerce, the Exchange's centre piece was a large reading room with an open hammer beam roof (now enclosed). The design was based on a Flemish Cloth Hall, with a series of tall, ornamented dormer windows, and a heavy tower at the eastern end, designed to be capped by an Oudenarde-type tower. Unfortunately, the Meadows sump won the day. The *Building Chronicle* watched in horrified fascination: **July 1854:** *This elaborate building, now drawing towards completion, has been undertaken to afford accommodation for the mercantile classes of Dundee.*
The nature of the foundations having been such as to require artificial means of security, Mr Bryce commenced with a layer of concrete 3

foot thick. *The insufficiency of this is already too evident: the front wall being some inches off the perpendicular, the inside arches slacked, and rents visible in various places.*

October 1854: *the sinking of the foundations at the new Royal Exchange in Dundee has now become so serious that further operations on the Tower have been suspended.*

. . . **December 5th 1854:** *The Royal Exchange still stands in statu quo, an unfortunate object.*

June 1855: *At the Exchange, signs of an attempt to complete the Tower are at length visible. We believe the ornate upper part is to be wholly omitted, and a peak roof substituted to finish it off with as little additional weight as possible. The Police Commissioners have agreed to lower the street to suit the sinking — an unfortunate necessity.*

September 1855: *Our Exchange has been undergoing a brushing-up of late, after such a lapse of activity as made its completion almost despaired of. The Tower has been summarily stopped — we cannot say finished — with a pierced Gothic parapet immediately above the clock. The whole ornate spire contemplated in the original design is now sacrificed to the imperative prudence which forbids additional weight being put upon an insufficient foundation. The consequence of this, in an architectural point of view, is very damaging to the building. The operation which had been going on for some time — replacing the broken and splintered masonry produced by the late settlements, resembles nothing so much as the slapping and veneering of a shop front, and is a very unfortunate circumstance in the case of such an elaborate building.*

On the far corner of Meadowside and 11-15 Panmure Street, is the 1878 **BANK OF SCOTLAND** (formerly Union Bank) designed as a three-storey Renaissance pile by Alexander Johnston; who had, in 1872, also designed the central block across the street dignified (or squashed) by a gigantic Corinthian order.

The east side of Albert Square, has four buildings of interest: The **CALEDONIAN INSURANCE BUILDING,** 33 Albert Square, designed in flat-relief, American inspired, Jacobean in 1886. The architect, John Murray Robertson, had his own offices in these chambers which was his second major office building in the Burgh.

Next door, the **PRUDENTIAL BUILDING** was, of course, designed by Alfred Waterhouse and Son in 1895. Either Dundee or age was taming the exuberance of their English

The Royal Exchange Competition

Plans were sent to a number of architects throughout Scotland, the terms being that the usual commission would be given to the successful party. Some 6 or 7 designs were sent in and were exhibited in the old coffee room. The directors selected two, but subsequent discussion having shown that neither of these could be adopted with anything like unanimity it was resolved to compromise the matter by setting both aside. A commission was accordingly given to Mr Bryce of Edinburgh to prepare fresh plans, and these having been approved of, the work was proceeded with. The directors, without any obligation to do so, gave 20 guineas to the authors of the two designs referred to above, understood to be Mr Burnet of Glasgow and Mr McLaren of Dundee (the *Building Chronicle*).

Alexander Johnston had first surfaced in Dundee working for Peddie and Kinnear on the Morgan Hospital and Mayfield in 1869. Within a few years, he put up his own brass plate: the firm later becoming Johnston and Baxter, whose successor is Baxter, Clark and Paul.

The Caledonian and Prudential Insurance buildings, Meadowside.

Prudential buildings, so this is a more modest version of the house-style. *The Builder* noted that it was built *in the dull red bricks that seem inevitable even in towns where stone is the usual and natural material. The design is quiet and pleasing, with panelled pilaster strips flanking the windows, a good cornice, gables to the side bays.* Formerly it had tall arch-linked stacks. The glazed tile interior was designed by son Paul. Trying to be neighbourly in a modern way, the **HALIFAX BUILDING SOCIETY,** next door, is a 1975 building by Baxter Clark and Paul, grafted onto an indifferent modern shop. We no longer have the money to do gables as they used to but this attempt is a genuinely urbane recognition of the importance of Albert Square.

In its route north, Meadowside hosts, behind the Royal Exchange, the **PEARL BUILDING** designed in 1898 by the quarrelsome engineer/architects Charles and Leslie Ower, sons of the Harbour engineer. Much of the detail is from the hand of W. G. Lamond, in red sandstone Flemish, before Lamond discovered the sinuous joys of Art Nouveau.

Further up, the route toward Victoria Road provides the former **JUTE INDUSTRIES BUILDING,** a sandstone severe, island building by James Maclaren 1886, the headquarters of the mighty Cox Brothers. Opposite is **BONAR HOUSE,** a 1928 building by Robert Gibson, gifted by George Bonar as a School of Economics to provide business and management training, eventually to be absorbed into the university. Turning left, 25 along Bell Street, may be found **INDIA BUILDINGS,** 86 Bell Street, J. Murray Robertson's first Dundee solo commission: an 1876 homage to Glasgow's Alexander Thomson in its precise sculptural detailing, which deserves cleaning; although wholly lacking Thomson's ability for creating picturesque massing.

26 Westward along Bell Street may be found the **INSTITUTE OF ART AND TECHNOLOGY,** 40 Bell Street, 1907 whose front was won in competition by J. H. Langlands, the School Board architect, with the distinctive hand of W. G. Lamond. The architect's contribution was really a new front for a building already commissioned from the engineer Robert Gibson (see Bonar House above): and the result is a large, symmetrical building with central pediment and projecting wings enlivened with eccentrically gigantic baroque details.

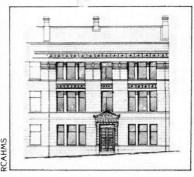

top: The Halifax Building Society. *middle:* The strongly Greek Thomson-influenced India Buildings in Bell Street. *above:* The Institute of Art and Technology.

McKean

27 The **HIGH SCHOOL,** Euclid Crescent, by George Angus, 1834, is the only significant piece of Beaux-Arts planning in Dundee: the High School was designed as the visual termination of Reform Street. The subsequent, steadfast, refusal to undertake any further similar planning has left the High School marooned in an educational enclave with none of the spatial setting that might have been to its advantage: it is not part of Albert Square, although contiguous with it. The project was for a single building, entitled the *Seminaries* which brought into one place Dundee's three schools: the Academy, the Grammar School; and the Kirkyard School. The Burgh Council raised finance from its locally levied Ale and Beer Tax, and organised an architectural competition — at the time very much in vogue in Edinburgh. Competitors included Archibald Simpson, the classical Aberdonian architect, and George Smith, who had designed the Exchange Coffee House. The competition was awarded to Angus, with the instruction that he include the advantages of his competitors' designs. The Seminaries comprise a major, ashlar, Greek revival building well worthy of comparison with Edinburgh's Royal High School, (if lacking in the colonnades, and the substructure which gives the latter such presence,) dominated by a splendidly pompous, eight-column Doric portico.

THE AMALGAMATION of the three Dundee schools in one building led to an educational *disruption* in the Burgh when the Dundee School Board claimed rights of appointment. In order to forestall a major crisis, Baillie William Harris offered the School Board £10,000 to found another school on condition that they respected the High School's independence, with which they built Harris Academy (see p. 80). Harris also gave the High School £20,000 topped by another great Dundonian benefactor, Sir William Ogilvy Dalgleish, partner of Peter Carmichael in Baxter Brothers.

McKean

Adjacent to the High School, is the 1889 Frenchfield **GIRLS' HIGH SCHOOL,** designed by J. G. Fairley for his ex-partner Alexander McCulloch who was a civil engineer. Fairley had American connections, and the building has the kind of distant French echoes, high roofs and richly sculptured attics much favoured by Canadian and American millionaires. There is a fine hall and stair, with notable Art Glass. Nearby, just down Euclid Street, is the **DUNDEE HIGH SCHOOL** annexe, formerly a Savings Bank, in distinctive Gothic with original details, by James Maclaren, 1867.

above: Girls' High School. *below:* 1a West Bell Street. *bottom:* Sheriff Court.

McKean

28 The **REGIONAL MUSIC CENTRE,** 1a West Bell Street, by James Black, 1840, is one of Black's few surviving designs. Originally a church, this corner, classical building has great elegance. The raised ground floor is rusticated, the upper storey is pilastered with blind panels, and there are balustrades on the roof. It was designed as the end pavilion of a never completed neo-classical terrace, whose aspirations crumbled with the 1881 arrival of the **CURR NIGHT REFUGE** by Ireland and Maclaren, and the matching **PARISH COUNCIL CHAMBERS** of 1900 by William Alexander, the City Architect.

29 The **SHERIFF COURT BUILDING** West Bell Street, is a neo-classical building by George Angus, 1833, with portico and wings, most of which is actually the work of William Scott, 1863, including the square courtroom albeit to Angus' designs. Only the eastern screen wall and pavilion survives from the Angus work. The Doric portico and round headed

PSA

windows are not untypical of a mid century Edinburgh bank. The **SALVATION ARMY HOSTEL,** Court House Square, by Charles Edward, 1851, was originally designed as an industrial school, with affinities to a Tudor Manor house: a plain, two-tone stone block, with sharp gables and a thin tower. Edward was a local Clerk of Works made good into architecture, and after about 1865 most of the work became carried out by his partner T. S. Robertson.

The **METHODIST CHURCH,** 15 Ward Road, by David Mackenzie, 1866, is Gothic in painted rubble, which Mackenzie, as the designer of the Ward Road block between Rattray Street and Nicoll Street, also adapted to normal Presbyterian business chambers. Just behind, up Nicoll Street, may be seen David Baxter's peculiarly Glaswegian **FORESTERS HALLS** 1900, with red stone towers flanking a rather fine vaguely Art Nouveau entrance. **1-7 WARD ROAD** is an 1869 three-storey block of warehouses and offices, again by Edward with an unusually arcaded ground floor. Just round the corner in Constitution Road is the **WARD CHAPEL CONGREGATIONAL CHURCH,** a simple rectangular church with a facade in plasterer's perpendicular, by J. Brewster, 1833.

RIAS Library

above: Original drawing of the Foresters Halls. *below:* The General Post Office.

McKean

30 Virtually opposite, is the **GENERAL POST OFFICE,** Meadowside, a confident building of classical detail by W. W. Robertson, 1898 — balustraded, string coursed and columned, culminating in a mini-Florentine duomo on the corner.

On the opposite corner, filling a gusset site, [31] is the even grander **WARD ROAD MUSEUM,** designed in the year of the triumph of his grand plan for Dundee, 1911, by City Engineer and Architect James Thomson. It is a Baroque building, of the type that the best London architects were using.

McKean

above: The Courier building and the Albert Institute from The Howff. *below:* The Ward Road Museum.

City of Dundee

[32] **THE HOWFF,** Barrack Street. In 1564 Mary Queen of Scots granted the lands formerly used by the Greyfriars, and lying outside the Burgh boundary to the north, to the Council for use as a graveyard since that of St Clements was overcrowded and insanitary. The Howff, which earned its name (meeting place) from the curious fact that the Dundee Incorporated Trades met and dealt their business amongst these intimations of mortality, subsequently garnered a collection of funerary monuments of a quality second only to Greyfriars Kirk in Edinburgh. The west wall retains huge, deep, blind arcading of 1601, (whose award-winning restoration was carried out by the City Architect's Department as part of an MSC programme), comparable to that which used to line the ground floor of Provost Pierson's house in the Grassmarket. Still enclosed by high walls or railings, graced with mature trees, overlooked by grand Victorian monuments and lined on one side

by the curving, cobbled Barrack Street, the Howff epitomises the heart of Old Dundee.

Across the road, **FRIARFIELD HOUSE,** by James Maclaren and G. S. Aitken, 1873, was designed as the office block for the now demolished Ward Mills. Mostly plain, it has a curious tower on the corner containing a circular entrance hall, the roof sliced off French style. Just south of this is the brasher **WILLISON HOUSE** on the corner of Willison Street, designed c. 1934 by H. Pearce Robbie, of Findlay, Stewart and Robbie. It is a faience-faced furniture shop with Art Deco motifs around the doorway that must have looked much brighter in the days when this area was a thriving centre. Across the desolation, the west side of north Lindsay Street is still a fine sight, particularly the austere, gigantic **HALLEY BROTHERS** factory designed with plain venetian windows by Harry Thomson in 1911; and **KEYHOLE,** part of the *Lindsay Street Works,* by Maclaren and Aitken, 1874. It is a mad, grotesquely over-exuberant, French Cathedral, with a steep roofed, oblong tower, whose tall, gabled front with a rose window in the attic conveys just a hint of St Denis.

THE HOWFF TOMBSTONES, monuments, sarcophagi and sacrament houses date from 16th-19th centuries and are notable for the quirkiness of the inscriptions. The Victorians claimed to spot the following:

J. P. P.
Provost of Dundee
Hallelujah
Hallelujee

Here lie I
Epity Pie
My husband
My twenty bairns
And I

The Albert Institute contains a 19th century volume detailing all inscriptions then decipherable.

McKean

51

[33] NETHERGATE

McKean

The ancient route from Dundee ran north-west from the Market place, past the Luckenbooths, up the Argylesgait (later Overgait) through the West Port, along Hawkhill and out. The Nethergate (originally Fleukergait) was the route linking the properties with a river frontage back to the centre; only later did it become linked to the villages of Westfield and Springfield, to join the Perth Road at the Sinderins. The class in Scots communities usually moved westwards, and so it was in Dundee. The scale of this ancient thoroughfare can still be appreciated despite the Angus Hotel and Inner Ring Road, if viewed eastwards from the lounge of the Queen's Hotel. Beyond the hotel, the late Georgian residential character of the street, becomes apparent — *the site of elegant or flaunting homes of the elite of the town; and, along with its branch streets, has quite an aristocratic air. . . . The houses now stand apart, environed with lawns and flowerpots.*

Dundee District Libraries

top: The tower of St Mary's in 1846. *above:* The Town's Churches, immediately prior to the disastrous fire in 1841. *far right:* The G. G. Scott proposal for completing the crown on St Mary's.

[34] **THE TOWN'S CHURCHES,** consist of **ST MARY'S TOWER** (or Old Steeple) c. 1460, Samuel Bell's **STEEPLE CHURCH,** 1787, and the TOWN'S CHURCHES by William Burn 1842-7. The original parish church of Dundee was St Clement's, on a site now occupied by City Square. St Mary's, founded in

thanksgiving by the Earl of Huntingdon outside the City boundary, became the Town's predominant church by reason of its quality and scale, work beginning after 1442-3, the tower being perhaps 20 years later. It was the broadest non-cathedral church in Scotland, and the spectacular tower is unmatched anywhere in the country, the nearest competitors — pallid by comparison — being those of Stirling and Linlithgow. We may infer from the tower, its richness of carving and detail, something of the former town's churches prior to their sixteenth-century destruction by *our auld yenemies of England* and their obliteration by fire in 1841; and something of the wealth of the medieval mercantile community of Dundee. The tower, now a museum, is built of large blocks of varyingly coloured sandstone, the cynosures being the great, round-headed twin western doorways; the half-oval oculus with beautiful tracery set in the wall above, the doorway; the internal groined vaulting; the details of riches and buttresses; and the lacy Gothic parapet at the top. All that we see is a careful restoration by Sir Gilbert Scott badly scraped in the 1960s. The roof structure demonstrates that a crown like that of St Giles was evidently intended, but nobody can be certain if it was ever built.

The English had burnt out the nave: and the town converted the transepts and choir into three separate churches, leaving the steeple, as Pennant reported in 1772 *a magnificent Gothic tower, venerable and superb, now standing by itself*. In 1787 the Town instructed its architect, Samuel Bell, to rebuild the nave as a separate church called St Clement's, which he did in a feeble *heritors' Gothic* style, redeemed internally by the quality of the woodwork. Thomas Hood the nineteenth-century satirist and editor of *Punch* stayed in Dundee in 1814-15 to recover his health, and was tickled by the prospect of four churches in one building:

And four churches together with only one steeple, is an emblem quite apt for the thrift of the people.

In 1841, a boiler stoked up for a cold night began a fire, which annihilated the old church choir and transepts; its progress here described by the architect James Maclaren: *Nothing could equal the frightful fury of the devouring element — it ran with the speed of lightning along the base, the galleries, the rafters of the church, at one moment a brilliant white*

SIR GEORGE GILBERT SCOTT proposed a reconstruction of the alleged crown. In 1901 the opinion of the celebrated architectural historian Dr Thomas Ross was sought concerning the campaign to build it. *It is most lamentable to all who really take any practical interest in our national antiquities to find that nothing is safe from interference,* he replied. *The medieval architecture of Scotland is a closed chapter in our history, and we are not justified in altering or giving it an entirely different colour simply because we think it should have been something else, and it pleased the builders of the tower to finish it in the way we now behold. The fact remains that the architect of this tower had both (a crown termination and a cape-house termination) before him as is shown by the indications left for finishing it with a crown form, and that he deliberately decided in favour of the cape-house. I believe the proposal now is to remove the cape-house and put up the dreadful design prepared by Sir G. G. Scott some 30 years ago. We have enough of his work in Scotland already.*

line of light shot through the apex of the roof. After a moment of suspense, the flames burst with irresistible fury through the beautiful Gothic window facing the street in an intense mass of inconceivable brilliancy, carrying with it every portion of mason work. . . . About half past six the conflagration was at its height . . . the crashing of the galleries as they yielded

above: William Burn's drawing of the inside of the new Town's Churches. *below:* The west entrance to St Mary's Tower.

successively to the flames, the fall of ponderous roofs which shot volumes of fire into the air accompanied by dense clouds of embers — the sharp reports of stones splitting from walls and pillars resembling the discharge of artillery — and the frequent explosions which proceeded from the base of the buildings, contrived to create impressions of the most powerful and alarming character.

William Burn, appointed to rebuild, proposed to repair the old fabric of which a reasonable quantity survived. Unemployment in the building trade stimulated a lobby in favour of complete reconstruction, which Burn carried out with considerable skill, in a polished form of Gothic, with plaster vaulting in the transepts, rebuilt as a single church; and elegant St Giles derived arcades and timber ceilings in the choir which retained its original dedication to St Mary's. The Town's old **MERCAT CROSS,** in the kirkyard, consists of a modern reproduction of the Unicorn by Scott Sutherland RSA in resin-bronze, on top of John Mylne's 1586 carved shaft.

35 **DRAFFEN'S** now Debenhams, by T. H. Thoms, was completed in 1935 and is an American-style, framed building whose stone facings are supremely elegant. It does not pretend to be neo-classical, as was typical with other buildings of this structural type. Instead, it is designed as a vertical stone box transformed

by the way that the height of the building is punctuated by the second-storey stone balcony and the fine gargoyled, fourth-storey cornice; by the skill with which the stone has been laid and dentilled and, surrounding the windows, is layered back to create a deep reveal.

below: Whitehall Street and the Gilfillan Memorial Church. *bottom:* Draffens shop.

36 WHITEHALL STREET and CRESCENT.

R. Keith and others 1885-9. This second major area of Improvement Act road building, cleared some of the most historically insalubrious parts of Dundee. William Kidd, the publisher of Dundee guides 100 years ago, who was one of the first to occupy the palatial new buildings on the west side, described the district as *narrow, steep, dingy and dirty . . . the courts and dark passages were receptacles of filth . . . always pervaded by offensive effluvia, sometimes so strong as to be sickening. It was in such localities that fever and death walked arm in arm, and contributed largely to the silent population of the Howff.* Couttie's Wynd still survives as a back passage between Nethergate and Yeaman Shore, a lone survivor of earlier times. The *glory of modern architecture* in which the younger generation was expected to rejoice was commissioned by Kidd from his friend Robert Keith in a style *ornamental Gothic of a very handsome appearance.* Keith was really a mason, transformed into a tenement designer and a man of few design motifs — most Gothic. The

Wishart

above: Union Street. *below:* The tower of Green's Playhouse.

Wishart

overall design of the street had been, as in Commercial Street, produced by Mackison, the City Engineer and James Hutton, his assistant. At the Whitehall Crescent end of Debenham's the former Thomas Justice furnishing house has stylish interior work by W. W. Friskin 1937-38.

Terminating the vista at the bottom, and the centrepiece of Whitehall Crescent, is **GILFILLAN MEMORIAL CHURCH,** designed by Malcolm Stark in 1887. The Rev. George Gilfillan was a Dundee notable, celebrated for his fights and controversies, as well as for his preaching. He was a social reformer, partly responsible for the establishment of the asylum at Hawkhead, Paisley. He befriended William McGonagall and published a sumptuous, two-volume set of the works of Robert Burns. Had he been alive today, he would have been a television pundit. His following was enormous and his memorial church appropriately lavish — although now lacking its timber cupola. It has a square, worldly elevation, symmetrically disposed with vigorous baroque details around the doors and windows.

[37] **UNION STREET,** based upon William Burn's 1824 recommendations was designed by David Neave in 1828. Like Reform Street, it provided shops with handsome Georgian flats above, some of which survive with good plaster work and panelling. Together with South Union Street (now vanished) it was a long street of four-storey stone buildings — all now looking rather weather beaten. No. 11-19 is what remains of the **THISTLE HALL,** its grand windows and Ionic pilasters later incorporated into James Maclaren's Royal Hotel reconstruction. Neave had been the Town's architect, but suffered for his Riddoch connection, resigned in 1833, and got little work thereafter: an old-fashioned Tory in a radical town.

NETHERGATE CENTRE, designed by Hugh Wilson and Lewis Womersley 1975. The scale of this large, new, enclosed centre, the home of the joint District Council, Regional Council and Scottish Development Agency Dundee Project, is skilfully concealed from the Nethergate. It runs through the medieval long rigs to a much grander frontage on Yeaman Shore, and the architecture is defined by the crisp use of masonry like blockwork, symmetrically placed windows, and the elegant mansard-like roof. Those able to visit the upper offices, or those walking along the side access, will see the rear of other Nethergate buildings, some of which display clear historic fragments and traces of their predecessors.

38 **GREEN'S PLAYHOUSE,** designed by John Fairweather in 1936, is one of the few survivors of Dundee's 28 cinemas. Green's is an enormous building whose opulent, corinthian colonnaded interior by John Alexander of Newcastle has (according to cinema historian David Atwell) *standards of luxury unequalled anywhere else in Scotland.* Green was a Scots entrepreneur who completed but two of a projected series of such palaces: this, and the even larger version in Glasgow to which this is second in size amongst cinemas in Europe. The original, finned, tower survives underneath its new coating of grey, ribbed metal, composed to bring its image more up to date, but which still preserves the striking silhouette.

39 **ST PAUL'S, NETHERGATE,** Charles Wilson of Glasgow, 1850. *Of no great merit* claimed *The Builder,* yet the tall, thin spire of this church and Green's tower next door march well together, and its Gothic revival facade lends some detailed quality and interest to the street facade. It is virtually on the edge of the Inner Ring Road chasm, instead of being — as it was designed — an integral part of terraced buildings. Across the crossroads, a corner building against its will, is **132-134**

40 **NETHERGATE,** an elegant 1873 tenement built for Provost Don, designed with Venetian first floor windows and elegant chimney stacks by Young and Meldrum. Next door begins the odd terrace of **MILN'S BUILDING,** 136-140 Nethergate, possibly designed by Samuel Bell in 1790. It is a block of late Georgian, crudely detailed, speculative mansion flats built by James Miln, with bows to the south facing the river. It is the only block of this type surviving in Dundee, and would benefit from a wash and brush-up. Next door, **ST ANDREW'S ROMAN**

41 **CATHOLIC CATHEDRAL,** 150 Nethergate, an 1835 effusion by George Mathewson presents a somewhat unconvincing perpendicular style facade in stone and pinnacles. *The Builder* dismissed it as *churchwarden's gothic,* but it has more presence than that — if more like a chapel than a Cathedral. The interior is surprisingly impressive, the square box being divided by arcades into 3 bays, all focusing upon a raised, stepped and mystical apse.

Wishart

above: Miln's buildings. *below:* St Andrew's Cathedral.

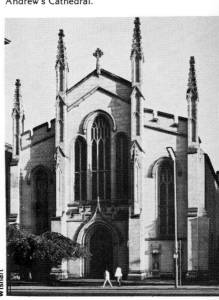

Wishart

42 **NETHERGATE HOUSE,** 158 Nethergate, possibly designed by Samuel Bell as the Town's architect, was built in 1790 for the celebrated Provost Alexander Riddoch, two years after he seized power in Dundee; power which he exercised single-handedly (or so claimed his opponents) until 1819, when he lost office following his defeat over the Harbour Bill, and a petition to Parliament over the way the Burgh was being run. The House, now a Bank, is a plain, elegant, laird's house, with single-storey symmetrically placed pavilions on each side, facing front garden. It is graced with an Ionic doorway, and slightly bowed windows. The views south, to the river, are spectacular.

Historians of Dundee are ambivalent about Riddoch. On the one hand, his drive, and skill in modernising the Burgh and his sagacity in preventing riots during the revolutionary period are admired. On the other, his ruthless extermination of all political opposition gave rise to a petition by many of the leading citizens, laid before Parliament in 1819, which revealed the true story: *The government of the town for the last century has passed from the hands of one absolute dictator to those of another: and at this moment the uncontrolled* power is vested in the person of a leader (Provost Riddoch) *who has held the situation for nearly forty years — generally excluding from the Council the more wealthy, independent and intelligent burgesses of the town.* The Parliamentary Committee established to consider the petition, and the other astounding submissions, condemned Dundee, noting in its report *of all the persons admitted into the Council under the present influence, only four have been natives of Dundee* (for Riddoch had dealt speedily with opposition, importing outsiders where necessary;) as a consequence of which, the above-mentioned petition recorded sourly *this Council's decisions have always been unanimous.* The Committee continued *One member of the Council (the Provost) had seventeen different transactions with the Town Council in the purchase and sale of property; and most of these transactions were for property in the line of new streets planned under the direction of the Council . . . .* The architect James Maclaren, writing in 1874, pointed out that the accusation of mixing private gain with public benefit was *an allegation not infrequently made in similar circumstances at the present day.* W. Norrie pointed out that despite Riddoch *promoting his private interests to a quite incredible extent,* Dundee had received Crichton, Castle, and Tay Streets, and the widening of Nethergate *all without imposing a shilling of local taxation on the inhabitants.* Norrie was also shrewd enough to realise Riddoch's real fault was as that, as shown in the Harbour debacle, *his management of the Town's revenues has been characterised as niggardly rather than judicious, and it has been questioned whether due means were employed to increase the income as well as keep down the expenditure of the Corporation.*

It was possibly the legends that clustered around Riddoch that damned the burgh in outsiders' eyes. For, taking Lord Cockburn as an example, many could only believe the worst: in **Circuit Journeys,** he wrote in 1844 *Dundee, that palace of Scottish blackguardism unless Paisley be entitled to contest this honour with it.;* and in 1852 he added *Dundee certainly now and for many years past the most blackguard place in Scotland. Dundee is a sink of atrocity which no moral flushing seems capable of cleansing.* A trifle exaggerated, perhaps. Dundonians were maybe less adept than those in other towns at concealing what they were doing.

43 The **QUEEN'S HOTEL,** Nethergate, designed by Young and Meldrum in 1878, is *as Gothic as pointed arches to the windows, recessed with little columns in them, and wooden barge-boards to the dormers can make it* wrote **The Builder.** It is on a corner site, the corner being chamfered, the main building being four storeys high, capped by a three-storey French attic. Inside, one may perceive the remains of a splendid oaken stairwell disguised in Fire-Officer protection, and the fine, first-floor corner lounge with its exceptional plastered ceiling and fine view down Nethergate.

44 In its current form, the **MORGAN TOWER,** 135-139 Nethergate, by Samuel Bell, 1794, is an immensely solid block of mansion flats, notable for its five-storey bow which projects

above: The Queens Hotel. *right:* The Morgan Tower.

The QUEEN'S HOTEL's air of not quite credible Victorian opulence is borne out by its history, an object lesson to architects wishing to take advantage of the new opportunities of being permitted to become developers. Young and Meldrum, acting upon information that the new Caledonian Station would be at Seabraes, built this hotel as Dundee's equivalent of Edinburgh's North British. Their inside information must have been wrong; the railway company took the station further into the Town, and the entire venture was financially disastrous, Andrew Mackie Meldrum ending up as an assistant in the family sports shop.

into the pavement providing Dundee's only townscape experience of the kind. It is pierced by a series of wonderfully vulgar Venetian windows, and capped with a Saracen's hat roof, with a Muslim moon as a weathervane. Tradition has it that these oriental features were at the request of its original sea-captain owner, Morgan. The thickness of the walls, the survival of huge blocks of red sandstone at the rear, the survival of a well and a peculiar U-shaped building behind the adjacent terrace; together with an early and persistent legend that Morgan converted rather than built his tower; and the knowledge that this corner of Dundee was at the far western extremity within the Town of 1548; all lead to the possibility that the history of this corner may be more complicated — and interesting — that the accepted theory of late eighteenth-century development.

SOUTH TAY STREET was laid out from 1792 through the grounds of Dundee's hospital, creating a new north/south link between Hawkhill and Nethergate. Most of the buildings are considerably later, the east side being Dundee's best surviving classical terrace, designed by architect David Neave, 1819-29, who lived here. Nothing like the scale, say, of Edinburgh's New Town, these pleasant three-storey houses are of Dundee's poor stone; they lack the raised, rusticated ground floor, of Edinburgh's streets; but some retain pleasant ironwork balconies; Ionic pilastered or columned doorways, in pairs; and good fan-light windows.

top: The Dundee Repertory Theatre.

below: The Caird Rest.

The cynosure however, is the **DUNDEE REPERTORY THEATRE,** by the Nicoll Russell Studio, 1982, a bravura composition of modern architecture. In form it is a large rectangle in light concrete blockwork, with its square facade punctured to open the inside to the outside. That is achieved by glazing this facade and projecting through it a cantilevered staircase winding up to the first floor and gallery. This deliberate merging of inside and outside is carried through into the detail of gravel on both sides. In contrast to the brightness of the blocks and the green transparency of the glass, the architects have deployed dark stained timber poles, triangles and boarding. Once inside the glass screen, all front-of-house spaces are interlinked in a circular route to provide a sequence of varying places each with its own character ranging from the restaurant, the sitting area, the bar to the foyer and the gallery.

The remaining houses on the south side of the Nethergate, **Nos. 162-172,** lining what was the cliff edge down to the Tay, are all of the late eighteenth century, contiguous, cramped, wealthy merchants' houses. Number **164,** possibly by Samuel Bell, dates from 1785, and sports a Venetian doorway; **166** an 1818 mansion probably by David Neave, has a projecting central bay, and an exuberantly rolling keystone above a delicate fan light. The **CAIRD REST,** 170-172, 1840, is a formal mansion with an Ionic porch.

62

Stanley Turner

⁴⁶DUNDEE UNIVERSITY

The establishment of University College in the elegant Regency suburbia of Hawkhill, screening the better part of town from the worst parts which lay directly to the north, had a consequence to Dundee comparable to that in London from the arrival of its much grander University in the Regency terraces of Bloomsbury. Dundee's college founded in 1880, and opened in 1883 as an adopted daughter of St Andrews and, from 1890, joined with the latter under the title of Queen's College was largely the result of the £120,000 bequest from Miss Baxter. The Technical Institute followed soon afterwards, in 1888, in neighbouring Small's Wynd — again upon Baxter munificence — that of Sir David. The College began by utilising what it found on site: a site that has gradually digested Park Place, Small's Wynd, Park Wynd, Airlie Place and if one includes the College of Art as part of the whole, Hawkhill Place and Springfield. One may spot here and there villas, engulfed by departments, overshadowed by monuments and linked by later buildings, the most self contained of which are on **UNION MOUNT,** (the Departments of Economics and Accountancy)

Geddes Quadrangle. *below:* Union Mount as it was at the turn of the century. *bottom:* Original drawing for Geddes Courtyard.

University of Dundee

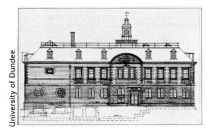

University of Dundee

Turner

Wishart

top right: The Bonar Hall. *above:* The Arts Tower. *below:* The Scrymgeour Building.

Stanley Turner

mostly 1818 and probably by David Neave; both with a slightly projecting, pedimental central bay, one with portico and the other (eastern) a porch with most ususual, foliated capitals that should have been Ionic. Just to the east, **BONAR HALL,** lining Park Place is a quality arrival of 1975 by Gillespie, Kidd and Coia, in orange brickwork and dark boarding originally planned as a part of a larger complex including the Theatre behind. It is very chunky, set low in the site and emphatically horizontal. Inside, the two foyers are joined by an elegant staircase à la Mackintosh. Also in Park Place is T. M. Cappon's great red sandstone pile built as a Training College (1911-12) and now the **SCRYMGEOUR BUILDING:** a lump of Institutional Renaissance now bereft of its cupola, and possibly influenced by Dick Peddie's County Building in Dumfries: its scale much more impressive if facing open land opposite as in the original architect's perspective. Between Park Place and Small's Wynd lies the **ARTS TOWER AND LIBRARY,** an early building (1961) by Robert Matthew Johnson-Marshall and Partners. It also provides the Senate Room, the Staff Club, and tutorial rooms. Given the dominance of hard-edged towers, this one is humane by contrast, the tower's slender gable to the street, and the bulk considerably lessened by the use of balconies and dark brown boarding. Facing the short, narrow, Small's Lane is the **SCHOOL OF MEDICINE,** a large (too large for the street) building sketched out by J. Murray Robertson and built by his successor James Findlay with turrets at the corner and a shallow, projecting entrance bay. Rather more dominant is the **GEOLOGY DEPARTMENT,** formerly the Technical Institute, in Small's Wynd, designed by J. Murray Robertson in

University of Dundee

left: The Technical Institute. *above:* Details of the facade panels. *below:* Belmont Hall. *bottom:* Detail of Carnegie Physics Building.

Spanphoto

McKean

1866. Internally, it is a wholly institutional and much altered, save for the spacious central stairhall. The exterior, however, catches the eye for its combination of heavy square severity, and extravagant (if shallow and not easily perceptible) detail, some picked out in different coloured stone. Influenced by the American architect H. H. Richardson, the Institute has a thin projecting, peculiarly pedimented central bay, the detail of which includes a mixture of Greek Thomson and sunburst motifs within a grandly symmetrical panelled pattern: an exercise in skilled facade composition. An insignificant path past more academic clutter leads to the real heart of the campus, the **GEDDES QUADRANGLE,** part of the **PHYSICS BUILDING,** designed by Rowand Anderson and Paul in 1909. It is the only survivor of the much grander scheme by the same architects; the quality of Geddes' courtyard making one regret the lack of its bigger brother. The north and west buildings in deep red stone with black dressings are in an energetic variation of late seventeenth and early eighteenth century Scots, with a tall Tolbooth-like tower. The quality of invention is best seen in the south gable of the western building which is wonderfully carved and pedimented, within which a Venetian window is treated with irreverence by the insertion of bull's eyes. The planting in the courtyard is of

E

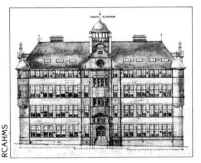

Davies

RCAHMS

top: Biological Sciences. *above:* School of Medicine. *below:* Airlie Place and the Tay.

oasis-like quality suitable to the memory of Sir Patrick Geddes who was once Professor here. Two buildings lying to the north, off Hawkhill may be noticed: **BELMONT HALL,** by Gauldie Hardie Wright and Needham, 1962-65,whose generous standards, quadrangular layout and careful design were much influenced by contemporary developments in Denmark. It represented *the last flicker of the belief that some introduction to graceful living was a function of University education.* The **BIOLOGICAL SCIENCES BUILDING,** by Mackie Raysay Taylor, 1968, is a large, muscular medieval fortress in white concrete propped up on great splayed legs, the horizontally varied fenestration being appropriately similar to that of modern hospitals. Gazing blankly down **AIRLIE PLACE,** itself a fine, short 1846 street of stone, terraced house, the west side by J. Dick Peddie amalgamated into Airlie Hall of Residence, is the glass wall of the **STUDENT ASSOCIATION BUILDING** by James Parr and Partners, 1973. On one level, it is the box approach to architecture taken to its most refined levels, perched above a stimulating red brick plinth, itself well set up on a platform at the end of the Place. On another level it is a much more sophisticated way of enclosing in one formal shape, disparate activities such as a swimming pool, bars, meeting rooms and games rooms. The nearby **CHAPLAINCY CENTRE** is by the same architects in the same year. Further west, facing Perth Road, can be

McKean

found the Crawford Building of the **DUNCAN OF JORDANSTONE COLLEGE OF ART;** a competition winning scheme by James Wallace of 1937, the building was delayed by the War, and, when finally built in 1950 onwards was considerably altered from the original. It is a fairly large slab, unfortunately set back from the road, with details typical of the period — large windows, mediocre brick, and thin concrete framing. The character of its neighbour, the **MATTHEW BUILDING,** designed by Baxter Clark and Paul in 1974 is of an altogether different order: an example of the *Brutalist* approach to architecture whose interior quality is as high as can be found anywhere else in Scotland. A subtle use of the concrete frame allows views from one floor to the next, deep lightwells, a sense of contrasting spaciousness and enclosure: in short a good example of fine, inter-related spaces of different character. If there is a problem, it will be that a building of concrete and blockwork may prove to be too finite a structure for the constantly evolving patterns of Art Schools. Across the road, number **150 PERTH ROAD** is a late eighteenth-century house enlivened by a first-floor venetian window and heavily rusticated door surround, all detailed in a particularly untutored manner.

top: Student Association building: *above:* Matthew Building, College of Art.

McKean

THE FIRST SUBURB
48 MAGDALEN YARD

Magdalen Yard had been vested in the Council from early years, as witness the following Council extract of 1679: *Annent the Keiping ginerall Randivois at the Magdalen Yard, the Councell appoynts one generall randevouse to be keiped at the Magdalen Yeard of all the fancible men within this brugh, between sextie and sexteine to be holden on Thursday nixt.*

Turner

Roseangle/Magdalen Yard was a low-lying peninsula into the Tay before the shore-line of the Tay was evened out by successive reclamation schemes, beginning with the Esplanade, and soon followed by the railway, a by-pass road and a growing airport. Its name may derive from a link with a medieval monastic dependancy, the Victorians recording the finding of carved stones at the bottom of Step Row.

It became Dundee's first self-contained suburb, downhill from the Nethergate, villas being built on Perth Road, Roseangle and the Yard. In later times, the steep slope down from Perth Road became built up with crowded housing and industry; and the final blow to its privileged status was struck by the arrival of the railway and the conversion of the shore at Seabraes into marshalling yards. The formation of Magdalen Green into a public park was undertaken by Provost Alexander Lawson in the early 1840's specifically to relieve the severe unemployment caused by *dull trade* and the consequent threats from Chartists. The foreshore was thus transformed into a large recreation area which by 1879 had become *a place of resort much frequented by the west enders* for cricket and other games recognised by the erection of its fine cast-iron **BANDSTAND** in 1889. They also came to see *one of the most gigantic works of mankind,* the Tay railway bridge.

The first **TAY BRIDGE,** designed by Sir Thomas Bouch, was a single track, lattice girder bridge finished in 1878.
That bridge and its fate provided the raw material from which William McGonagall first made his name through his apostrophes to the Tay Bridge, the Tay Bridge disaster, and the New Tay Bridge, which he observed from his room up Paton's Lane. McGonagall began as a handloom weaver in a mill up the Scouringburn until made redundant by the introduction of machinery. Teaching himself from a set of *penny Shakespeares* (which accounts for his archaisms), he became one of the world's most famous bad poets, prepared to address any contemporary event in the manner of seventeenth-century popular Bab Sheets and Balladists. Dispensing with such poetical tools as rhythm and structure, McGonagall concentrated solely upon rhyme, using a popular language appropriate to his popular recitations of his works, by which he survived.

Beautiful Railway Bridge of the Silvery Tay
With your numerous arches and pillars in so grand array
And your central girders which seem to the eye
To be almost towering to the sky

• • •

I hope that God will protect all passengers
By night and by day
And that no accident will befall them while crossing
The Bridge of the Silvery Tay
For that would be most awful to be seen
Near by Dundee and the Magdalen Green.

top: The first Tay Bridge, the fateful High Girders at the centre. *middle:* Opening celebrations. *above:* The second Tay Bridge. *left:* Tay Road Bridge by W. A. Fairhurst & Partners.

69

Unfortunately, a combination of poor inspection, faulty castings, insufficient design loading and racing trains took their toll. During an exceptional gale on 28th December 1879, the high girders at the centre blew down along with the 5.27 p.m. passenger train from Burntisland.

McGonagall rushed to print:

> Beautiful Railway Bridge of the Silvery Tay
> Alas! I am very sorry to say
> That ninety lives have been taken away

• • •

(the poet here expatiates on the Demon of the Air, Boreas, and the loud brayings of the Storm Fiend)

• • •

> I must now conclude my say
> By telling the world fearlessly without the least dismay
> That your central girders would not have given way
> At least many sensible men do say
> had they been supported on each side with buttresses
> . . . .

The **NEW BRIDGE** was designed by W. H. Barlow, with ironwork by Sir William Arrol, and completed in 1886 at just under double the cost of the original, whose designer, the unfortunate Sir Thomas Bouch, was by now dead.

McGonagall was ready for the new bridge, and had inspected its structure:

> Beautiful new railway bridge of the Silvery Tay
> With your strong brick piers and buttresses . . .

On the corner, as Roseangle descends from the main road, **ST JOHN'S CHURCH,** by James Hutton, 1884, is a striking Gothic silhouette with high quality details, and an interesting 1895 organ case by R. and J. Sibbald. As the road descends, it penetrates a district of great but decaying quality: substantial classical villas intermixed with industry and isolated tenements, with street names reaching back to a lost arcadia: Greenfield, Westfield, Seafield, Bellefield, Shepherd's Loan and Strawberry Bank. The majority of villas are substantially similar in design — two-storey stone buildings, occasionally embellished with a projecting central bay, or pediment, columns by the entrance, roof projections, fanlights and balconies; or a combination of these. Most have mature, dank stone-walled gardens which help to define the streets; and with the exception of eighteenth-century Westfield

St John's Church

RCAHMS

The Vine

House, most date from 1820-40. Numbers **22, 41 and 61 MAGDALEN YARD ROAD** are of this sort. The only coherent development is in **MAGDALEN PLACE,** designed in the 1830's by George Mathewson as a select development of late classical villas with Doric Columns: it is a short north/south cul-de-sac rather too tightly laid out. Undoubtedly, the best single piece of architecture is **THE VINE,** 43 Magdalen Yard Road designed by an unknown architect — maybe from Perth — in 1836, as part Art Gallery, part house for the art collector MP George Duncan; he who, by the magnificence of his Court dress, upstaged the entire Town Council on the arrival of the Queen in 1844. Now the Regional Medical Officer, whose office this is, has some of the finest classical detail in Scotland. The house is a square pavilion, set up on a plinth within a garden for the views to the estuary, whose interior is focused upon a dome-lit hall pillared with Ionic columns. The neo Grecian composition, with its high-quality incised stonework, the battered (ie spreading out toward the bottom) windows, and the projecting entrance has significant similarities to Thomas Hamilton's Arthur Lodge, Dalkeith Road, Edinburgh.

Just round the corner, **THE SHRUBBERY, 67 Magdalen Yard Road** is an unspoiled villa of 1817 by David Neave, one of a pair, with a notable Ionic doorway and pediment. The **INSTITUTE FOR THE BLIND** occupies the land between Paton's Lane and Step Row; a small-scaled though large Tudor collegiate development by Alexander Johnston, 1885, with Gothic poor-house overtones. **STEP ROW** contains a discreet development of 44 new harled and pantiled houses and flats by the Scottish Special Housing Association in a series of pleasant courtyards. The entire district, however, is dominated by the bulk and campanile of the **SEAFIELD WORKS,** the 1861 mill of Sanderson, Thomson, Shepherd. **1-6 WINDSOR PLACE,** next door dates from 1835-40 and represents one of Dundee's finest neo-classical terraces: simple two-storey stone houses, topped by a continuous balustrade, the central portion and the wings slightly projecting. The rhythm of the Doric columned porches is also neatly designed to achieve symmetry for the whole terrace: continuous across the entire front of the end houses; the central two houses having their porches twinned into a single portico.

1-28 WINDSOR STREET, with 1872 frontages by James Maclaren towards the top, presents a splendidly confident terrace of houses running down from Perth Road — the view from the top being not unlike similar in Brighton or Hove, (save there stucco, here stone) pleasing proportions, good Renaissance details round the windows and doors, and capped by balustrades.

Dundee District Library

THE SECOND SUBURB
CHAPELSHADE AND DUDHOPE

For the purposes of this guide, Chapelshade and Dudhope is taken to refer to that area north of the Inner Ring Road and sandwiched between Lochee Road and Hilltown, on the south slopes of the Law. Traditionally, however, Chapelshade referred to a much smaller area on the eastern side: that part for which a plan was drawn up by David Mackenzie in 1833. Contemporary quotations make it clear that building up the slopes had begun before that, for in 1824 it was noted that the district *had been subjected to the same irregularity of plan and building which seems endemic among those of the inhabitants who have it in their power to make themselves comfortable if only they could bear to communicate some portion of the same to their neighbours.* In the event, Mackenzie's select residential layout covered only two horseshoe layouts, and very quickly Chapelshade, like the rest of Dundee was invaded by factories and foundries. In medieval times, the entire area was part of the demesne of Dudhope, and this description begins on the western edge.

DUDHOPE CASTLE, 1580 onwards, is a splendid baronial survival dramatically set overlooking the City. In its current form it has two wings enclosing a courtyard, a turreted tower at each corner and a pended entrance flanked by decapitated drum towers. The great medieval keep visible in the Slezer view (p. 8) was taken down in the seventeenth century to render the building symmetrical around the entrance capped, as it is, by a bellcote set astride a corbelled pediment. The castle was the seat of the Scrymseours (or Scrimgeours), Hereditary Constables of

McKean

above: Constitution Terrace; principal survivor of David Mackenzie's Chapelshade layout. *top:* Dundee from Lochee Road in 1803, Dudhope Castle on the left.

Opposite: Windsor Street (top) and Place (bottom). Step Row (upper middle) Seafield Works (lower).

73

Rodgers

The Royal Infirmary was, at the time
of construction Dundee's largest
public building which may account
for a style and details which verged
on the ridiculous. Patrick Allan-
Fraser, the artist who remodelled
Hospitalfield, near Arbroath (Sir
Walter Scott's Monkbarns) gave the
following perceptive critique of the
building at a public lecture in 1854
prior to the hospital's opening: *It is
merely an imitation of an English
baronial residence consistent with its
exterior form. This building, besides
two long octagonal towers in front
and the usual profusion of gables
common to the style, has two large
pretentious towers one on each of the
two sides of the main building. Now
in really old Elizabethan houses,
towers were not erected for ornament
merely, but were considered
necessary additions to the internal
accommodation . . . those two
towers standing so prominent and
claiming to be considered principal
features are really of no service in
respect of their not affording any
additional useful accommodation.
They are four storeys in height. The
first three merely serve to prolong the
passages beyond where any passage
is required, and the fourth storey
although apparently intended to serve
some useful purpose, are not
furnished with doors or any openings
by which they could be entered.*

Dundee, from whom it passed to John
Graham of Claverhouse, the compelling anti-
hero of Sir Walter Scott's *Old Mortality.* After
passing to the Duke of Douglas, it was used as
a woollen mill, then reroofed and converted in
1799 to a barracks and now to a storehouse.
Originally it had a dormered profile. Daniel
Defoe thought it a *noble and ancient pile* over
250 years ago: it remains such and, if restored
and floodlit, would greatly add to Dundee's
attractions. The City's other hillside
monument is the enormous **DUNDEE ROYAL**
53 **INFIRMARY,** Barrack Road, by Coe and
Goodwin 1853-5, the core of which is a great
neo-Elizabethan pile with a central gatehouse
of an Oxbridge College sort, flanked by
octagonal towers with a corbelled oriel
window. Scotland's fascination with towers is
satisfied by a central one above the gatehouse
terminating in a cupola. The Infirmary, which
replaced the original in King Street
(immediately transformed to model lodgings
and now demolished), was the first building to
separate medical, surgical and fever wards.
The £14,000 raised for the Infirmary largely
by subscription, proved to be inadequate, the
building subsequently being the cause of a
claim for additional payments by the builder.
In February 1855 the *Building Chronicle*
reported, with some glee that *now that the
building is finished the Directors are at a loss
what to do with it, the unusually healthy
condition of the town and the enormously
expensive accommodation of the new buildings
being rather striking. It is accordingly being
offered to the government as a hospital for sick
and wounded soldiers.*

74

Down Barrack Road, at the Constitution Road corner is **GARLAND PLACE,** designed in 1867 by William Alexander; an unusually high quality stretch of tenements with Gothic details; and just downhill, on the corner of Dudhope Crescent Road, is **ST MARY MAGDALEN'S EPISCOPAL CHURCH,** a tall but badly skinned church by Edward and Robertson 1867, with a flèche and an impressive interior.

CONSTITUTION/UNION TERRACES; PROSPECT PLACE AND LAUREL BANK, were laid out in 1851 to David Mackenzie's plan of two steep, cramped horseshoes. The Constitution Terrace houses are of the style of James Maclaren: they form Dundee's riposte to Edinburgh's Blacket Place, and are quite beautiful: villas and semi-detached villas of good stone, with dutch gables, finials, greek key balconies, high garden walls and mature bushes. **1-4 SOMERVILLE PLACE,** by James Black, 1830, is a tiny development of semi-detached, harled Regency villas with stone margins, some single storey with fan-lit doorways so far from the parent as to seem detached. No. 4 has particularly fine plaster and timberwork interiors. **1-3 DUDHOPE TERRACE** is a collection of rather imposing, small neo-classical, 1840 villas by George Angus with disproportionately heavy Doric porches. To the west, in its own grounds, lies **DUDHOPE HOUSE,** an 1850 replacement by Charles Wilson of a classical predecessor: vaguely baronial in style and mostly disguised by a conservatory.

Uphill, the south slopes of the Law are cut into further terraces ranging from simple Victorian cottages facing unmade roads at the top (eg Adelaide Place) to much grander

houses downhill (eg Panmure Terrace). Of particular note are **10-11 ALBANY TERRACE** with its Italian Tower by Young and Meldrum 1877, another similar in Panmure Terrace by William Alexander, 1882; a typically eccentric, gothic house at number **8 PANMURE TERRACE** by Scotland's answer to William Burges, Frederick Pilkington, of 1872 and **DRUMBEG,** 3 Panmure Terrace by E. Tough and W. G. Lamond, 1909 — which has the quirky Art Nouveau touches one would have expected. There are some details in **No. 2 PANMURE TERRACE** which recall those of the Vine. **THE HIGH CHURCH,** Kinghorn Road by Ireland and Maclaren, 1879 provides a vague roughly detailed Gothic landmark on the skyline when seen from the Bridge: the **WAR MEMORIAL** on the top of the Law is a winning 1921 design by Thomas Braddock of Wimbledon, the assessor being Sir Robert Lorimer. Downhill to the west, at Gardner Street, Lawside, are the soaring gables of **ST** 54 **JOSEPH'S CONVENT OF MERCY** designed by A. MacPherson in 1892 as a *higher grade school for 60 young ladies.* Of all the Gothic buildings in Dundee, this more than most conveys by its austere massing, tall but thin proportions with quality details, the nearest to a genuine feeling of history.

top: 8 Panmure Terrace. *above:* St Joseph's Convent. *below:* St Mark's Church.

THE WESTERN APPROACH:
PERTH ROAD AND BLACKNESS TO NINEWELLS

Dundee has one of the finest entrances of any city in Britain. Perth Road, running along the sea ridge, lined on both sides by great houses, mature trees, stone walls or fine terraces is an asset that would be difficult to price. After leaving the University precinct, it passes through the compact, mainly eighteenth-century shopping street by the Sinderins prior to breaking out into Victorian villadom. Blackness Road rises higher up and, until the junction with Blackness Avenue, belongs to the north-west. Thereafter it, and everything else south of Balgay Hill, remains part of the western approaches. In general, the greater houses were those nearer the water's edge, becoming smaller as they go uphill.

55 **ST MARK'S CHURCH,** 158 Perth Road, by Pilkington and Bell, 1868-69, has much of the hard-edged vividness that characterises Pilkington's finest church — the muscular

Barclay Church in Edinburgh. This fine church in two-tone stone is on a corner site, displaying two facades in heavily articulated, Germanic detail. Some detailed similarities with Pilkington's house in Panmure Terrace may be perceived. **2-32 SPRINGFIELD,** 1828, is Dundee's finest Regency development, terraced houses with Greek Doric Porches and crowned by balustrades. **RYEHILL CHURCH,** being converted into flats, is by George Shaw Aitken, 1878, and significant principally for its grand, gabled facade to the street comprising a florid tracered window.

ST PETER'S CHURCH, St Peter's Street, was designed by the builders, the Brothers Hean, 1836, its general proportions and plain simplicity ennobled by the tower and stone spire against the east gable. Adjacent, in Ryehill Lane, is a fine gable mural painting depicting the history of Dundee by the Edinburgh Artists Collective which won a 1983 Art in Architecture Award from the Saltire Society. On the other side, at the corner of Pennycook Lane, is **HAWKHILL SCHOOL,** a stylish 1892 building by J. H. Langlands, with Renaissance-derived details, a balustrade, and oversized urns. Uphill amidst tenements and industrial units is **ANNFIELD HOUSE,** 5 Annfield Street, which, dating from 1793, is one of Dundee's earliest surviving classical suburban houses. Note the shallow 3-bay, central bow lined with the remains of a superb cast-iron balcony. It could look splendid if restored. Just round the corner, in **PEDDIE STREET,** Dundee District Council Architects, and Bell and Farquharson, have been rehabilitating the severe, late Victorian, tenements.

ST JOHN'S CROSS CHURCH, Blackness Avenue, Frank Thomson 1911-14. Great, stone, Romanesque and cruciform, one of Dundee's many unfinished churches. Robbie and Wellwood's 1974 extension is appropriately blank, in douce brick and jagged mono-pitch roofs. The Cross Church was burnt out of the Town's Churches in 1841, taking over the Gaelic Chapel in Tay Street before removing here. It is thus one of Dundee's oldest and most influential congregations, and the chosen design is more sternly appropriate than the Wrennish classical and Gothic alternatives preferred by the architect. Just downhill, on the corner of Perth Road, is Frank Thomson's 1904 **BLACKNESS LIBRARY,** designed for his father from his

Wishart

above: St Peter's Church. *below:* Annfield; Springfield; and St John's Church.

Wishart

Dundee District Libraries

Dundee District Libraries

London digs, one of a pair he was designing at the time. Also in red stone, it is a severe two-storey Renaissance building with great Ionic columns, with a fine eliptical staircase well within. The sculpture is by Albert Hodge. Across the road, the tenements **1-5 BLACKNESS AVENUE** designed by James Maclaren from 1868 are among Dundee's best examples with bay windows, carvings, pilasters and heavy string courses. Save for the harsh, plain tenements for the poor, Dundee is largely devoid of this building type which flourished so well in Edinburgh and Glasgow in the late nineteenth century. By contrast, as Blackness itself demonstrates, Dundee has one of the most extensive — pro rata to its population — collections of individual or semi-detached houses in Scotland, leading one commentator in 1912 to compare the wide Victorian and Edwardian streets and avenues of Blackness to a *garden city*. The 60 **McCHEYNE MEMORIAL CHURCH,** 328 Perth Road, by Pilkington and Bell, 1870, commemorates the celebrated minister of St Peter's, the first encumbent of the post, aged 23, associated with the religious revival. He became involved in Evangelical missions, but, health failing, he died aged 29. The Memorial Church is suitably splendid, in the florid Gothic that distinguished Pilkington's work.

61 **SEYMOUR LODGE,** 259 Perth Road, by Charles and Leslie Ower, 1880, is a formidable corner mansion with huge, bargeboarded gables and soaring roofs capped by chimneystacks. Once the home of a celebrated ladies school *drawn from the best local families,* this formidable Gothic horror is the kind of high-Victorian fantasy of the kind favoured by American horror movies. The Owers were also responsible for the similar houses, five years later (1885) along Perth Road at the bottom of Hyndford Street and Rockfield Street.

The remainder of Perth Road and its environs are a combination of great houses or public buildings beginning with **BINROCK,** no. 456 Perth Road. It is a late eighteenth-century two-storey villa with a projecting bay, fanlit doorway and stable block; skilfully touched up by Mills and Shepherd at the turn of the century. In 1923 the estate was put up for sale, within whose grounds Patrick Thoms designed four houses, the last, in 1929, being

top: McCheyne Memorial Church.
above: Seymour Lodge.

GREYWALLS, for himself. It is the only one
constructed entirely of stone, possibly
because, as a result of the demolition of the
Vault at the time, plentiful stone was
available. The resulting character, from the
south-west, is one of a low-lying Cumbrian
manor house set snugly into the hillside, with
stone chimneys and stone slates. The plan of
the western end of the house is forked like a
Y, leading to twin gables between which, at
ground level, there is a loggia and, at first
floor level, a balcony between two of the
bedrooms. In both loggia and balcony, there
are fine wrought-iron hooks from which the
architect used to suspend his hammock.
Inside, the idiom is Arts and Crafts, although
the leaded window panes were features chosen
not by the architect, but by his wife. The
timber work is excellent, the chimney places
in the drawing-room and the hall both have
ingle-nooks, and the principal bedroom has a
white coved ceiling.

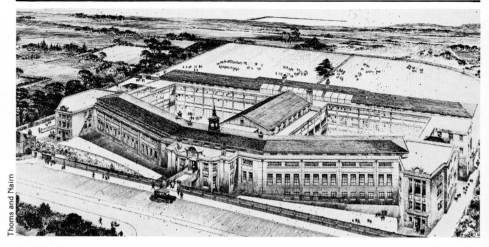

Thoms and Nairn

Walker

top: Competition winning drawing for the Harris Academy. *above:* St Helen's, Perth Road.

The following acid comment from the **Building Chronicle** in 1855 might have been written just about St Helen's: *Now in North Britain we have old Scottish — thanks to Burn and Billings' Baronial Antiquities — taking its place as, par excellence, the style of 9/10ths of our domestic buildings; and oh! what oddities are being perpetrated in its name. The grim bastion towers of Caerlaverock and Craigmillar are being revived in the retreats of peaceable country gentlemen; heavy battlements surmount their doorway and loopholes command it.*

63 The **HARRIS ACADEMY,** a 1926 competition winning design by Donald Ross of Thoms and Wilkie, uses the slope to present a single storey building to the road, but a two-storeyed building downhill, The wings are swept back on either side of the entrance which is dominated by a cupola and reached by a drawbridge. Across the road, the Western 64 Cemetery presents a fine Gothic screen wall and gateway delicately detailed by J. R. Findlater, but so damaged by lighting that part resembles a decayed tooth.

65 **ST HELEN'S,** 474 Perth Road is an 1850 effusion by Charles Wilson of Glasgow. Unlike Dudhope House, this is a really vigorous neo-baronial bankers palace, despite some classical details: the towers, crow-stepped gables and string courses all point to the influence of Robert Billings, whose *Ecclesiastical and Baronial Antiquities of Scotland* were being published.

TAY PARK, 484 Perth Road, is another baronial structure with a 1916 wing by Thoms and Wilkie. Uphill, at 3 Norwood Crescent is **BALLOCHMYLE,** J. Murray Robertson's own little house designed in 1880, complete with his leitmotif of the flattened stone tower with 66 an ogee roof. **THE BOREEN,** 6 West Grove Avenue, by Thoms and Wilkie, 1911, is a beautiful house, Cumbrian rather than Scots, rubble built with dressed stone quoins, and projecting bays — like a miniature Arts and 67 Crafts manor house. **HILL RISE,** 21 Farington Street, also by Thoms and Wilkie three years later, is rather more sophisticated. The modern house on the corner of **ARNHALL**

RCAHMS

GARDENS by Lowe and Barrie, 1936, is one of Dundee's few, good "moderne" houses. It sports the white walls, flat roof, corner windows, and cut-away corner for a balcony that distinguished this style. The building is possibly best seen from Arnhall Drive, below, 8 of which number **5 ARNHALL DRIVE** is a plain house enlivened by fine Art Nouveau railings designed by W W Friskin for himself. Friskin was responsible for a number of inter-war churches and schools, the crafted brick of his 1938 chapel in Graham Street being an appropriate memorial. **NYOORA,** 514 Perth Road, is an elaborate red sandstone Scots villa by Thoms and Wilkie 1905; less appealing than others for, despite its superbly crafted stone and interior plasterwork, it is rather more frigid. Nearby, **WESTDENE,** 506 Perth Road, a Tudor-styled villa by Watson and Salmond, 1903, has been altered by exchanging mullions for picture windows. **DUNCRAIG,** 3 Glamis Road, is a late building (1890) by the Ower brothers in the same baronialised Gothic horror style of Seymour Lodge.

Wishart

9 **ARDVRECK,** 516 Perth Road, is a design of 1907 by Mills and Shepherd in a part of Dundee that seemed to be a Thoms and Wilkie fiefdom. With its sloping roofs, beautiful stone, and stone mullions, and gigantic, asymmetrically planned semi-circular arch enfolding the garden door, this house must be one of the finest Arts and Crafts houses in Scotland. The **UNIVERSITY**

Thoms & Wilkie

top: The Boreen. *Middle:* Arnhall Gardens. *above:* Nyoora. *below:* Ardvreck.

81

F

Dundee University

Thomas of Nairn

top: Botanic Gardens Pavilion. *above:*
369 Perth Road.

below: Balgay House.

McKean

⁷⁰**BOTANIC GARDENS,** off Burnaby Street, whose original 1973 buildings are by Thoms and Wilkie, provide a beautiful oasis with fine views over the Tay; dramatically enhanced by the new, 1982 pavilion designed by Arkos Design Partnership. The more sedate **VERNONHOLME,** next door, was designed by David Baxter in 1910: now Health Board offices, it is a fairly typical, heavy, Italianate classical villa (none of the wayward invention of Thoms and Wilkie) distinguished by its principal entrance recessed behind a 3-bay, double columned loggia. On the other side of Perth Road, is **DUNCARSE,** 1858, another plain mansion by Charles Wilson, well set up on a plateau overlooking the river, with a superb, later conservatory which encloses the entire porch. The person for whom it was built — George Armitstead, later Lord Armitstead, was a Russian merchant from Archangel who married a Baxter; whose family duly arranged for his election to Parliament despite the fact he spoke but little English. He is commemorated by a series of annual lectures. On the very outskirts, by Hazel Avenue, may be found **INNISCARRA,** 385 Perth Road, a red roofed, two-storey house in Cape Dutch style by W. Williamson, 1905; and the **HIRSEL,** 389 Perth Road, designed by Thoms and Wilkie in the same year. Also in Hazel Avenue is **NARRACOORTE,** a modest 1952 house with all rooms on the first floor and a fine two-storey stair window, designed by Gauldie Hardie Wright and Needham. It shows typical open-planning of the period, and an early use of under-floor heating. Just down **RIVERSIDE CRESCENT,** can be seen the surprising timber-framed bay window of the Nicoll Russell Studio conversion of a standard 1970's home.

The upper parts of Blackness provide even more spectacular views over the Tay as well as a number of items of interest. The demesne was that of Balgay House, one of Dundee's older and larger lairds' houses, once lived in by the Morgan of Morgan Hospital. The estate (and house) is now the **ROYAL VICTORIA** ⁷¹**HOSPITAL** with Balgay Hill and Victoria Park being acquired by the Corporation in 1870 as public parks. The Mills Observatory, on the top of Balgay Hill, was added in 1930. **BALGAY HOUSE** still survives at the centre, c. 1760; clearly a douce laird's mansion, pleasantly proportioned, with a shallowly projecting, pedimented centrepiece. **16 KELSO STREET,** is a good pair of semi-detached "moderne" houses of the 1930's, complete with metal framed, horizontally proportioned curving bay windows. The **APPROVED SCHOOL,** Blackness Road is an appealing (to outsiders) French chateau, with Dutch gables on the wings, designed by James Maclaren and Son in 1896. Nearby, **365 BLACKNESS ROAD** is a small house with Arts and Crafts details on the stonework and well-sculpted chimney designed around a two-storey octagonal, top lit hall, designed by W. Gauldie in 1924. At the corner of Blackness Avenue and Glamis Road is the **MYSTERY HOUSE,** an unexceptional building save for its story. In 1919 James Thomson, the City Architect proposed to the Council that they should invest in a prototype house, testing new materials, methods and services for the proposed Council house programme. Some time later, a Councillor enquired as to the result. The house built with the money was the Mystery House: and its occupant, James Thomson. **GLAMIS DRIVE** is worth exploring for a series of tantalising glimpses of large houses of varying dates well concealed by high walls and luxuriant foliage.

72   The cynosure of Ninewells, now, is **NINEWELLS HOSPITAL,** designed by Robert Matthew Johnson-Marshall and partners, completed in 1975. It is more like a medical New Town, so large is the development; and it was the first completely new teaching hospital built in Britain. It makes an interesting comparison to the same architects' later Stirling University campus. At Ninewells they were not so blessed with a beautiful site. The resulting building is neat, white, horizontally proportioned; best viewed from Invergowrie, where the contrast between the massive tubed chimney and the white horizontal blocks set into the hillside is seen to good effect.

above: 365 Blackness Road. *above:* Ninewells Hospital.

Wishart

THE NORTH-WEST APPROACH

The ancient north-west route to Coupar Angus, ran almost immediately into rough and hilly countryside such that in the early nineteenth century it was still risky to walk unaccompanied from Dundee to Lochee. This part of Dundee was influenced by two principal physical characteristics: the first being the Scouringburn, and the second being the extraordinary explosion of the Cox Brothers' company town at Lochee. The Scouring burn is now underground, and no street bears its name, although the ancient western route of Guthrie Street to Polepark follows its line. The area between Lochee Road and Hawkhill attracted the greatest single concentration of mills and industrial buildings in the Dundee area, and swiftly became infamous: *there is probably not a more unsightly part of the town* said the 1873 Guide *from the combination of closely packed mills, and miserable unwholesome dwellings than that which stretches to the south of this once delightful "Pleasance";* and in 1912 the City's Housing Convener noted that the squalid conditions of the medieval *rookeries* had been *emulated by the modern crowded tenement, elbowed by the mill and jostled by the factory relieved from which the worker vanished into an adjacent close or pend* drawing particular attention to the aim that, by developing Craigie in garden-city layout *along the happier ideas of our time, such districts as that lying between Lochee and Hawkhill can never be repeated.*

This is now designated the **BLACKNESS BUSINESS DEVELOPMENT AREA,** and subject to major renewal in a joint regional and district project led by the Scottish Development Agency. Industrial buildings are either repaired and re-used, or replaced by modern factory units of brick and curved, wriggly metal roofs.

THE DA VINCI PUB, Henderson's Wynd, by Alan Phillips, 1980, is the idiosyncratic conversion of a small industrial shed into a pub: it is very stylishly modern inside and out, making a change from tartan carpets and plasticised oak; instead the name is in neon, the corners are cut away with ziggurat-shaped windows, and topless classical columns flank 73 the doorway. The **TAY WORKS,** Lochee Road, built by the Gilroy Brothers, mid 1850's-1865, forms the entire western edge of Marketgait between Lochee Road and Guthrie Street, and has a massive classical, grim, splendour, enhanced by a magnificent pediment with carved sculptures. The construction, like most other later Dundee mills is jack-arched, for fire-proofing reasons, and the iron roof trusses in the central loft are a superb example of Victorian engineering skill.

The grandeur was only to be expected as the Gilroys were a manufacturing dynasty second only to the Baxters and the Coxes, and the image of the Tay Works had to be as grand (and externally was grander) as the Dens; just as the Gilroys' house in Broughty Ferry, Castleroy, had to be no less grand than the rival — Carbet Castle, belonging to the Grimonds.

The 1870's **SOUTH MILL,** in Brown Street, and the more interesting, and much earlier **VERDANT WORKS,** Mill Street, (dating from the 1830's) displaying a cornice, a courtyard plan, and a chimney stack built into the walls of the works unlike the later free standing ones, are both worth a glance. Nearby, in **DOUGLAS STREET,** a vigorous, arcaded, patterned brick warehouse still survives. Uphill, to the south, metamorphosed into a transportation depot in modern factory land, proudly protrudes the bellcote of the chapel-

McKean

above: surviving David Neave villa in Milnbank Road. *below:* The Coffin Mill.

Wishart

85

McKean

Parr

top: St Joseph's School. *above:* Balgay Road flats.

like church of **ST MARY MAGDALENE,** Blinshall Street, 1854, by imported architects Coe and Goodwin; who used expensive imported Caen stone for the dressings and imported the celebrated William Butterfield to design the tiled reredos. Of this scheme *The Ecclesiologist* wrote in 1855: *This very simple and cheap church appears to us to be more richly deserving of praise for what it aims at than the gorgeous and over-laden palazzo with which the architect so accidentally won the first prize for the Foreign Office in the Italian style.*

[74]Dating from 1828, the **COFFIN MILL,** further up Brook Street, at the corner of Horsewater Wynd, is one of Dundee's oldest surviving mills. Properly called the Logie Works, the mill earns its name from a combination of its odd, coffin-shaped site, and a grisly story of a mill lass whose hair was caught in the machinery. The mill, now redundant, has an elegant form, with a seven-storey flat capped tower on the corner, and ranks of Venetian windows on the south side ennobling the engine room. Two villas flanking Forest Park Road, but facing **MILNBANK ROAD,** (of which number 24 is still in good condition) are by David Neave, dating from about 1815. They preserve Ionic columns flanking a doorway with a fan light and pediment above. Facing Blackness Road at the same latitude is C. G. Soutar's somewhat frigid **LOGIE SCHOOL,** 1928, which is harled with projecting stone bays. Slightly downhill, across the Blackness Road is **ST JOSEPH'S SCHOOL,** 126 Blackness Road, designed by the School Board Architect J. H. Langlands in 1905-6, and now an annexe to the College of Commerce. His assistant, W. G. Lamond, (1854-1912) was the real designer, producing the Art Nouveau details, and the large arched windows to double volume classrooms. The stylish eastern addition is by W. W. Friskin, 1933. Immediately behind the School, in Wilkie's Lane, is the 1874 **CHURCH,** high on a hillock overlooking the city, designed by Alexander Ellis and Robert G. Wilson of Aberdeen; it is a plain gothic barn from the outside, but has a uniquely unaltered and atmospheric interior (should it ever be unlocked) with a huge 1900 reredos by Pugin and Pugin. Up Blackness Road, and spanning the valley to the north, can be found the **LOGIE HOUSING DEVELOPMENT,** begun 1919 and split by that typical 1920's innovation, a short boulevard (called Logie Avenue) going to and from nowhere. The houses are unspectacular

and would benefit from some brilliant whitewash; but the layout is curvilinear from "picturesque" as well as steepness reasons; the streets names are determinedly rustic — Ashbank Road, Lime Street, Elm Street and Sycamore Place — and the development was one of the first in Europe to have a district heating scheme. In cold weather, the pavements steamed like New York: (no longer: each house now has its own central heating). By Blackness Road and Balgay Road, a good brown brick block of flats by James Parr and Partners, 1972, fittingly terminates a row of tenements like a bookend. To the north, across the valley, rising steeply from City Road, is a small community centred around ⁵**CLEGHORN STREET,** very similar to the 1850's Colonies developments in Edinburgh. They are rows of douce, well scaled two-storey terraces with gardens front and back: in reality upper and lower flats entered from different ⁶ sides of the house. **ST FRANCIS FRIARY,** Tullideph Road, a 1933 monastery by Reginald Fairlie, is a real smack in the eye: crouched on its site as though embarassed by its lurid red brick, it is as alien to Dundee as a spaceship. Most of the money went on the monastery: the towering chapel planned by Fairlie had to be redesigned on a much lower and smaller scale by A. R. Conlon, but with the addition of a carved tympanum by Hew Lorimer.

above: Cleghorn Street. *below:* St Francis' Friary.

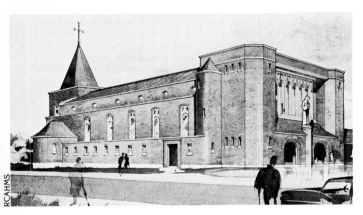

⁷⁷**ANCRUM ROAD PUBLIC SCHOOL,** Ancrum Road, looking down upon Lochee, is a 1904 remodelling by J. H. Langlands and the first school for which William Gillespie Lamond had responsibility: his spoor may be spotted in the projecting staircase with climbing slit windows, capped by a wavy parapet.

On the very edge of Lochee, standing high above the by-pass, is the rump of **LOCHEE STATION,** now converted into a club. Designed by James Gowans, 1860-1, an architectural and railway pioneer, the north wall of the station is well worth a glance, exemplifying as it does Gowans' view on modular design (everything designed in 2 foot units) and the panelling of his stonework.

Lochee: *above:* the Station. *right and below:* Cox's Stack, and the Camperdown Works.

LOCHEE

Lochee, about 1½ miles to the north-west of central Dundee owes its existence to the humble Lochee burn which powered its mills, and to neighbouring Dundee which acted as its market.

The reality is that Lochee was virtually a company town. Its beginnings date back to the arrival of a manufacturer called Cox in Locheye about 1700. By 1791, 276 handlooms were at work in Lochee most belonging to, or working for, David Cox. His descendants pioneered the manufacture of jute cloth in Britain, as Cox Brothers, with the 78construction of the **CAMPERDOWN WORKS** which, in its heyday, covered about 30 acres of ground and employed almost 6,000 people. As a result, the population of Lochee quadrupled between 1841-51.

The works, off Methven Street, were designed by G. A. Cox between 1861-8, on a truly gigantic scale: modern in layout, most of the floor space being single-storey, but with a giant sliver mill 70 feet high, almost one tenth of a mile long, with 100 foot tower with cast iron cupola at the east end.

The Works' greatest landmark, tall enough to rival the Law, is the 282 foot high patterned brick chimney added by James Maclaren in 1865-6, known as **COX'S STACK,** which acts both as beacon, and a grim reminder of a servitude. Maclaren designed the (superbly patterned) chimney as a jute-owner's reply both to Italian campaniles and to his rivals' pediments and cupolas downtown. It was the definitive statement of the Cox dynasty.

At the gates of the works symbolising, perhaps, the totality of Cox control, is the parish church of **ST NINIAN'S,** Methven Street, a plain box church by David Neave 1829-30, with two storeys of plain windows, shallow pilasters topped by a pediment, itself capped by a pleasant stone spire of a classical type. **ST MARY'S CHURCH,** 41 High Street, by J. A. Hansom, in 1865, is an exceptional building by a London architect who also founded *The Builder* magazine. A plain, pitched roof exterior is ennobled at the east end, by an octagonal, buttressed and prismatically-roofed chancel which also does duty as a spire. Inside, the atmosphere is mystical: a sense that the world outside is shut away by heavily enclosing walls, and by the superb detail and craftsmanship.

Wishart

Wishart

above: St Ninian's Church. *below:* St Mary's Church exterior and interior.

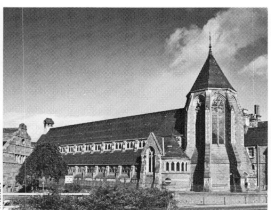

Walker

RIAS Library

right: Lochee Library and Baths. *below:* Clydesdale Bank.

Wishart

Just beyond the Church, up the High Street, is the **LIBRARY AND PUBLIC BATHS,** designed by J. Murray Robertson in 1894-6, paid for by the Coxs, and recently refurbished by Dundee Architect's Department. It is a lovely, red stone building with Jacobean details, string courses, panelling and gables. *One of the most satisfactory buildings we have noticed* thought **The Builder** in 1896. Moving up the High Street there are, besides the 1970's whitetiled shopping centre, three other buildings to notice: the **CLYDESDALE BANK,** 93 High Street, an 1876 corner building by C. & L. Ower: not in their American Gothic this time, but an equally rogue baronial style topped by vividly unnecessary corbels; the 1903 **SAVINGS BANK,** by David Baxter in his usual neo-Renaissance style; and James Maclaren's **LOCHEE WEST CHURCH,** 191 High Street, which had a Gothic facade and spire. To the west, the **LOCHEE CABINET FACTORY** at 127 South Road was a 1911 Thoms and Wilkie brick and stone effort in the Renaissance style: perhaps to suit the type of furniture made inside. To the east, **CLEMENT PARK,** Harefield Road, is another building by the Cox's architect Maclaren, in 1854, for the Cox's themselves: comprising the largest surviving jute palace in Dundee, its future safeguarded by nurses. A twin-towered, stone confection of variously plundered styles from thin medievalism to Carolean gables, it is, for Dundee, unusually close to t'mill. The **BEECHWOOD** housing scheme is a large 1936 housing development which won a Saltire Society Award in its day, but now requires imagination. Its brick and iron 1930's details are of some interest. North-west of Lochee, on the northern slopes of Balgay Hill, 80 is the enormous 1960-65 **MENZIESHILL DEVELOPMENT,** dominated by its five, fifteen-storey blocks of flats, one of the major post-war, overspill areas consequent upon clearances in the historic centre.

In 1756 only one house had a slate roof, the remainder being thatched cottages, and the *bonnet makers had all seats at the end of their houses where they sat and wrought their bonnets with large wires. The houses in general had the gables to the streets, but were only a ground floor covered with thatch, but many only with divots of earth . . . only a few of them had glass windows.* By 1834, the district was described as: *consisting of irregular ill-built houses, but interspersed with many manufactories where cloths are prepared, chiefly for the merchants and agents in the Wellgate and Murraygate, who send them abroad to the remotest corners of Asia and America.* By 1846, it had developed a *motley and squalid appearance* and, with a few isolated survivals, Hilltown underwent its second redevelopment in the nineteenth century, as tenements.

In 1912, the then City's Housing Convener condemned the tenements: *running in straight rows against the skyline, practically sunless in the ground flats, compelling the children to play, and the wayfarer to pass as if between two tall, draught creating and sun obstructing stone dykes, almost completely blocking out the fine views . . . Notoriously it presents all the conditions favourable to consumption . . . We can see the process of slum creation proceeding under our very eyes.*

HILLTOWN AND THE ROAD NORTH

Hilltown was the route north and east from Dundee, straight up a steep incline from the Wellgate. It was thus beyond the Burgh's regality and mercantile restrictions, and the Constables of Dundee, from their stronghold in Dudhope, saw no harm in letting their land be used by craftsmen in rivalry to those in the Burgh below. Being outside the walls, it was the area most likely to be sacked and burned by any army commander wishing to make a point without having to take on the entire burgh. Thus it was with the Marquess of Montrose; and thus also did it suffer at the hands of one of their own Constables, James Graham of Claverhouse in 1689. The route was never planned, and the building pattern was one of street frontages with long rigs behind, which later became courts, wynds and alleys, mostly populated by craft trades, as perpetuated in the names Bonnet Hill (Bonnetmakers) and Bucklemaker Wynd.

The most dramatic change was caused by the removal of the main traffic route with the cutting of King Street and the construction of Victoria Road through Bucklemaker Wynd to provide a gentler ascent to Forfar and beyond. The cottages were engulfed in a march of

above: St Mary's Forebank, original drawing; *top:* as it is today.

RIAS Library

above: Pilkinton and Bell's Victoria Street corner block.

factories, worthy churches and serried ranks of very plain tenements.

81 Hilltown's opening from Victoria Street is dominated by the extravagant corner block designed by Pilkington and Bell, 1877, whose encrusted Italianate corbels prop up an oversailing roof. Uphill, to the right, lies the Forebank area, the location of some yet surviving late eighteenth-century suburban houses. It is most notable for the twin 82 campaniles, of **ST MARY'S FOREBANK** church, Powrie Place. These two, 1900, turrets which combine echoes of hillside Tuscany with the most advanced Art Nouveau out of Glasgow, are the work of T. M. Cappon's assistant William Gillespie Lamond. The huge barn of a church, a late (1850) work by George Mathewson, contains an immensely rich, barrel-vaulted romanesque interior, whose muscular round-headed arches march toward the altar. The adjacent **POWRIE PLACE** housing scheme by the City Council's architects, 1981, is designed in two large blocks with low sweeping tiled roofs, so as not to obstruct views of St Mary's. Back at Hilltown, the **WINDMILL BAR** is an eighteenth-century survival incorporated into an 1868 stepped tenement block. The block at the corner of Hilltown and **KINGHORNE ROAD**, is a flashy shop front of 1934 complete with black marble and horizontal windows, designed by William Patrick. On the west side, is an extensive planned housing 83 redevelopment called Hilltown West, by the City Architect's Department together with (in

below: St Salvador's Church.

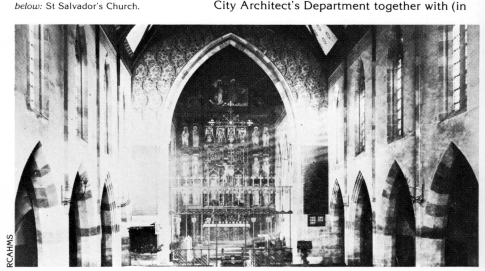

part) Bett Brothers. With its variegated roofscape, good landscaping and colourful choice of materials, it is part of Dundee's current trend toward a more cottage-like style of housing. What is yet to be tackled is the urban coherence of an ancient street and shopping centre such as Hilltown. The dominant visual features are the four twenty-three-storey blocks of flats in Maxwelltown, designed by Ian Burke, Martin and partners 1965-8. In St Salvador's Street, **ST SALVADOR'S CHURCH** is an early Arts and Crafts Church by G. F. Bodley in 1868 whose interior with its open roof, and sumptuously rich stencilled wall decoration, is of outstanding quality. Restoration began in the early 1970's by R. Snowden, under the direction of Colin McWilliam. Away to the east, may be found David Clunas' innovatory concrete houses in **COURT STREET,** 1875, currently being rehabilitated. It is uncertain what the Edinburgh City Improvement Act architect was doing in Dundee, unless it was to carry out experiments impossible in the capital. The houses, built for the Working Mens' Housing Association by the Concrete Building Company, have good proportions, cornices and mouldings: but the quality control during original construction now being revealed is little better than the first Tay Bridge. Adjacent Eliza Street houses **STOBSWELL GIRLS' SCHOOL,** 1907 another Langlands/Lamond design, which makes an interesting contrast with Clepington School, Sandeman Street just behind, also by Langlands, but designed in 1892 before he took on Lamond. It is a grand stone vision of

above: SS Peter and Paul. *below:* Stobswell Girls' School — original drawing by W. G. Lamond.

Coldside Library.

perceptible quality: but it lacks the unique flavour of the later building.

Due west, in Byron Street, is the brilliant scarlet brick complex of **SS PETER AND** 87 **PAUL ROMAN CATHOLIC SCHOOL AND CHURCH.** The school is 1929 by W. W. Friskin and quite attractive, with Byzantine details and good wrought iron, presumably to suit the 1928 church by Reginald Fairlie alongside. The church is barn-like, the interior being plain with round columns and a flat timber roof, with an oddly mystical, Byzantine apse.

88 Just round the corner **ROCKWELL CENTRAL SCHOOL,** Lawton Road, is also by Friskin, 1930: possibly his nicest — or at least friendliest: a purple brick with brick details, buildings arranged around central spaces.

89 **COLDSIDE LIBRARY,** 130 Strathmartine Road, was designed — like Blackness, by Frank Thomson, for his father, the City Architect James, in 1908. It is his best: a great concave-fronted Y-plan library with massive baroque gable facades facing Strathmore Avenue and Strathmartine Road. This elegant building is saved from being frigid by a blind upper storey in bright red brick.

THE NORTH-EAST ROUTE TO FORFAR

In 1871 a competition was held for a new road to the north-east, to replace the difficulties of Hilltown. The route chosen was along Bucklemaker Wynd, and the competition was won by George Shaw Aitken of whose buildings little trace remains. Victoria Road itself has been transformed from a stately, if grim Victorian route by the demolition of the south side to accommodate the Inner Ring Road; by the replacement of the urban street tenements by cheerful and colourful flats and

Provost Orchar and Provost Robertson designed, built and fitted machines for jute works, doing so well out of it that Orchar was able to donate the *Orchar Art Gallery* to Broughty Ferry. When the demand for machinery in Dundee slackened, they exported to America and to Calcutta: in so doing, they sold to the Indians the weapons the latter needed to process jute themselves: thereby pulling the bung out of Dundee's economy.

houses from whose pantiles and coloured harling one might infer a transplant from the East Street, St Monance, Fife (City Architect's Department 1978). The landscape design includes *tot lots* for children under 7. East Neuk transplants clearly work. This one earned both a Saltire Society Commendation and a Civic Trust Award in 1979. Survivors to be noted are: **60 VICTORIA ROAD** the works by Robertson and Orchar, built in 1874. It is a three-storey, baronial factory block with a 1921 marble staircase.

At 72 Victoria Road is the former **TRINITY CHURCH** 1877 by J. G. Fairley, in the French Gothic style, distinctive for its white stone, enormous rose window, and the fact that the building's entrance is between two Gothic shop fronts; symbolising — as for the rest of Dundee — the close connection in this city between religion and the rise of capitalism. Thomas Hood had satirised that, also, back in 1815:

> And their rooted dislike and aversion to waste
> Is suffered sometimes to encroach on their taste;
> For beneath a theatre or chapel they'll pop,
> A saleroom or warehouse or mean little shop

Trinity Church.

RIAS Library

Wishart

top: St Patrick's Church. *above:* Dens Road School.

Craigie Street housing.

Wishart

[91] **25 ARTHURSTONE TERRACE** is the now derelict factory of Malcolm Ogilvie & Co: a large two-storey building with projecting centre (minus pediment) carried on a series of storey-height arcades. Further along the Terrace is **ARTHURSTONE LIBRARY,** a red sandstone building with Renaissance details and an elaborate upstairs reading room by W. Alexander 1903; and **ST PATRICK'S RC CHURCH** at 3 Arthurstone Terrace, redolent of days when there was more money in this district, designed by T. M. Cappon in 1897, in red rubble, the tower capped by an octagonal belfry. The sinuous curving parapets above the confessionals is a trace of how W. G. Lamond had replaced Harry East as Cappon's assistant. Up **Dens Road** to the north-west, were the **BOWBRIDGE WORKS,** the 1857 flagship of another Dundee dynasty, the Grimonds, formerly entered through a magnificent gateway surmounted by a camel. In its heyday, the works employed over 3,000 people, and were noted for their *perfect equipment with the newest machinery and the best appliances.* The workers were provided with *a comfortable dining room, lavatories, a large hall for amusements and lectures.* Slightly further up again is the Langlands/Lamond [92] **DENS ROAD SCHOOL,** 1908, mixing Art Nouveau with Arts and Crafts details. **THE SAVINGS BANK,** Princes Street, is a 1914 effort by David Baxter in his Edwardian Renaissance style but with the unorthodox addition of a domed clock tower. The gushet of Dura and Albert Streets houses the [93] **OGILVIE CHURCH,** by Edward and Robertson 1876, which presents different faces to all winds. The square, slated, Scots tower (when seen from the west) turns out triangular (when seen from the east): details — particularly the decorative timber barge-boarding, are good. Morgan Street houses the austere **MORGAN PLACE,** a 1930's scheme by James MacLellan Brown, a stone courtyard development, with towers at the corners, makes a better attempt to create decent housing conditions within a genuine Scots sense of place than many subsequent efforts. Nearby in **CRAIGIE** [94] **STREET,** however, is a fine 1981 response to the same problem by the City Architect, using blockwork masonry, and taking advantage of lifts to create real towers, and a sense of occasion: its slightly castellated air, sheltering its own courtyard, and its much brighter colours indicate how Scottish urban townscape might develop in the future.

Founded by a nabob returned home, the history of the **MORGAN ACADEMY** is unusual. It was originally conceived as a Dundonian answer to George Heriot's Hospital in Edinburgh, for the education of 180 boys *the sons of tradesmen and persons of the working class generally whose parents stand in need of assistance.* The legacy for the Morgan Hospital was unexpected, and those who had had expectations from John Morgan challenged the will in the Court of Session, compelling Dundee's Nine Trades to fight to the House of Lords on behalf of the Burgh's interest. By the time they won and the will was proven, the substance had, (as in the celebrated Jarndyce v. Jarndyce case in Dickens' *Bleak House*) been reduced significantly leading to an initial foundation for only 60 boys.

The Academy, as it soon became, was designed in 1863-6 by Peddie and Kinnear, and is set on a balustraded terrace above a high slope overlooking Dundee. Its similarity to David Bryce's 1862 Fettes College in Edinburgh is quite remarkable, although the latter is much larger, considerably more rigorous, and in a much grander parkland setting. The Academy is symmetrical, the focus being the great central turreted tower, and the flanking wings with their Netherlandish gables. The totality is much more Dutch gothic than French, and were

The Morgan Academy

The governing regulations were strict, but included the following: *the more degrading kinds of corporal punishment shall be avoided or resorted to as seldom as possible and never for mere literacy deficiency if unaccompanied with moral blame.*

Walker

G

Madeira Street

Walker

Fettes not available for comparison, one would revel in the exuberance of Morgan's turrets, chimneys, dormer windows, oriels, and tracery. Immediately to the rear of the building, the northside of **MADEIRA STREET** is a row of idiosyncratic Gothic cottages, designed in the 1870's by the Rev. George Augustus Harris, presumably to sympathise with the Academy.

Completed by 1863, Dundee's sole, formal, 96 Victorian Park, **BAXTER PARK** was the result of a donation of £50,000 from Sir David Baxter and his sisters, who imported Sir Joseph Paxton in 1859 to advise on layout. Clearly nothing but the best would do. The upper end of the park is laid out formally, with the pleasant, Renaissance pavilion, forming the transition to the more open space downhill. The pavilion, with its loggia of twin doric columns, contains a niche for the marble statue of Sir David by Sir John Steell (1863), now removed to the Albert Institute, *the funds of which were subscribed by all classes of the population*. Opposite the south-east corner of the park, at 69 Dalkeith Road, is **ST MARY'S MANSE** by C. & L. Ower in 1890, another eccentric essay into red stone medievalism, the surrounding railings of which were central to the design. Five years later, the Owers inflicted another villa, **THE**

Baxter Park

Wishart

ANCHORAGE, on Bingham Terrace, this time rather less Gothic, and more seafaring as befits its name. There is an outlook on the roof, and the hall is Corinthian columned. The remainder of **BINGHAM TERRACE** is an oddity for Scotland: a terrace of American — or Muswell Hill — houses in a form of 1909 Edwardian not seen elsewhere in Scotland: designed by Edward Tough of Hutton and Tough, they have timber work balconies, verandas, turrets and the wall's external skin consists in places of harled expanded metal lath. At the end of Bingham Terrace, strictly in Craigiebank, is the **EASTERN NECROPOLIS** whose three-arched Gothic gateway in painted stone, with curving traceried screen walls, was designed in 1863 by W. Scott and D. Mackenzie.

The squat, castellated **DUNDEE WATERWORKS** on the corner of Stobsmuir/Clepington Roads is a 1908 essay by David Baxter in muddy Dundee stone. The **KEILLER FACTORY,** Lammerton Terrace is an ugly 1930-50's brick industrial box, worthy of notice as being a lonely survivor of another great Dundonian dynasty whose city centre works, behind the High Street, have given way to a shopping arcade. **53/55 FORFAR ROAD** is a curious pair of red sandstone, Art Nouveau, semi-detached bungalows by W. G. Lamond (designed in 1906) for his employer, J. H. Langlands. They have splayed walls, battered chimney, and Art Nouveau turrets, but lack the verticality that enabled the pure proportions of Art Nouveau to be realised.

top: Bingham Terrace. *above:* Forfar Road, the semi-detached bungalows designed by W. G. Lamond for his employer.

The Eastern Necropolis.

right: The Guthrie Mausoleum, Roodyards burial ground.

Wishart

THE EASTERN ROUTE ALONG THE SHORE

The eastern, coastal route from Dundee was the most historic, forming part of the trip from Aberdeen to Edinburgh. There are few survivals of ancient history, the inner parts being dominated by dock and industrial development; followed by the dominance of West Ferry, then the ancient fishing village of Broughty Ferry, leading through Barnhill to Monifieth. Each will be treated separately.

99/ The **ROODYARDS BURIAL GROUND,** Broughty Ferry Road, began as a receptacle for 1561 plague victims, but most of its monuments date from 1820-60, an exception being the late eighteenth-century Guthrie mausoleum. There is a catacomb by the rear gate. On the hill above is the former **GLEBELANDS SCHOOL** which enfolds another Langlands/Lamond school of 1911. 100 To the east is the enormous **WATSON STREET HOUSING** by the City Architects' Department which won a Saltire Society

Award in 1981. Although some of the tenements facing Broughty Ferry Road have been well restored, their typical Dundonian severity stands as a yardstick of what this new, colourful fishing-village has been attempting to get away from. The steepness of the slope, and the views over the Docks make such East-Neukery much more appropriate to this location. Along the slope beyond **SPRINGHILL** (once a celebrated villa location) are serried ranks of two-storey, cream painted concrete, flat roofed houses typical of the 1930's, each row peering out to sea over the ¹roof of those below. **CAROLINA HOUSE,** originally the Orphan Institution, designed on a cliff edge in 1870 by William Chalmers to replace the original in Small's Wynd, is a romantic Italian building with towers, turrets, wings, ironwork and blue-painted stonework: a downbeat public school which, in its original formation, it was.

²North of Stannergate lies the **CRAIGIE GARDEN SUBURB,** planned by James Thomson, and designed in 1919 by son Harry, on a concentric plan for *artisans*. The layout is the most interesting part of Craigie, its imagery lifted directly from Ebenezer Howard's *Garden Cities of Tomorrow* complete with church at the centre. The scheme included an early attempt to disguise small blocks of flats as self contained villas. The church, designed by Frank Thomson in 1931, was built in 1937.

The plan of the Craigie estate.

The celebrated engineer, Ove Arup chose the adjoining location of Stannergate for the landfall of his original high-level Tay Bridge; so that it could be linked to Kingsway and the regional road network. Dundee preferred a bridge for Dundee, obliterating its central area and Docks to cope with it: whilst Arup constructed a little footbridge in Durham of the sort he had in mind for the Tay: a footbridge which has won many subsequent awards for elegant design.

Carolina House, looking like a French château.

WEST FERRY

The Craigie Drive roundabout marks the beginning of West Ferry, at one time one of the richest suburbs in Europe. To here, and to the hills above Broughty Ferry came the *merchant princes of Dundee whose palatial mansions occupy every point of vantage on the rising ground.*

It is a mid-to-late Victorian suburb, with one or two older villas on the coast road: entirely different from the ancient fishing village of Broughty Ferry to the east, even though in the latter *elegant shops have sprung up to supply the population with all the necessaries and elegancies which a well-to-do population demands.* It is an area of few main roads, framed by high stone walls and thick mature trees. Of many houses, the glimpse of a Tuscan turret above a rounded coping will have to suffice.

In the 1930's, it was said that Rolls Royces were clustered more thickly in West Ferry than anywhere else in the United Kingdom, possibly because Robertson the taxi tycoon would consider no other make for his fleet.

Claypotts Castle: the first villa in West Ferry

Ancient Monuments SDD

13 CLAYPOTTS CASTLE, was erected by John Strachan in 1560-88, during the troubled period of the mid-century, symptomatic of which were the activities of the throwback predator, Henry Lovell of Ballumbie (see p. 115) who was terrorising the neighbourhood from the fastness of his castle just to the north. It is clear that Strachan's view was to erect a villa at which, in the words of Forbes of Corgarff: *thieves will need knock ere they durst enter.* The centre of the house is a simple, large rectangle, with two enormous circular towers attached at opposite corners, bristling with gun loops at ground level. As it now appears the Castle is the apotheosis of the Z-plan tower, its most striking external features being towers capped, as they are, with square oversailing attic storeys corbelled out from below. One (of four) dormer window head survives, decorated with a sunburst motif.The principal rooms would have been on the first floor, the ground storey being occupied by vaulted stores and the kitchen. It was built over a 20-year period which may account for clear changes in the way it was constructed. Ancient Monument, open to the public: Guide Book available.

14 The westmost villa of note is **CRAIGIEBARN,** Craigiebarn Road, designed by C. G. Soutar in 1911, in many ways more worthy of note than earlier houses. It is a Scottish version of an English Arts and Crafts manor house, rubbly with harling, boarded gables and a conservatory. Entered through a low archway and sunken porch, the house's interior opens up into large, bright rooms with good plasterwork, the finest being the living room running the entire length of the house with oriel windows giving out to the estuary. Just **15** behind, off **Gardyne Road,** is the **COLLEGE OF EDUCATION** by Thoms and Wilkie, 1974. Its clean-cut geometric shapes suit its site, and the theatre is superb. Just south, off Craigiebarn Place, is **THE WYCK,** designed in 1908 by Freeman and Ogilvy: a grand, harled, Arts and Crafts house with a sweeping red tiled roof. On the corner of **Ralston Road** and **16** Mount, is **SUNNINGDALE,** a white, flat roofed, 1933 house by Donald Ross of Thoms and Wilkie, whose fretted parapet suited the Algerian preferences of the client. Adjacent in Ralston Mount, is another 1930's fashion plate: brick and string courses, jazz glass, canopies, and a curved two-storey bow with horizontal windows. Also in Ralston Road is **BEACHTOWER,** by J. Murray Robertson, 1874,

top: Craigiebarn, a fine Arts and Crafts house. *middle:* College of Education. *above:* Sunningdale, Ralston Road.

from top: Northwood; Balnacraig; Lazarim; Claremont Lodge.

constructed like the houses in Court Street, from shuttered concrete, then masked with stucco and classical details. The larger houses lie generally, to the south of Strathern Road, 107 but **NORTHWOOD,** 1880-82, is a huge towered mansion, for the nabob Mudies by G. S. Aitken, whilst **HERMON LODGE,** by Charles Edward, of 1870, (thus one of the earliest of the Victorians) has a pleasant Italianate tower and spectacular domed conservatory. Vaguely parallel, one south, is Albany Road, of which no. 30, **BALNACRAIG** is yet another 1863 vintage, homage to Queen Victoria's Osborne House on the Isle of Wight: three-storey Italianate, flat topped tower lording it over a two-storey house, white painted margins, in the garden of which lies **LAZARIM,** a 1982 house by the Nicoll Russell Studio, a brilliant black-and-white house half of whose gable is glazed to the eaves, even the chimney stack and balustrade sharing the crow-stepped motif. At 5 Albany Road, is **THE CROFT,** a late 1898 house by J. Murray Robertson, whose brick walls are covered with trellis work. At the corner of Albany Road and 108 Grove Road is the entrance to **CLAREMONT,** 61 Albany Road, a great marmalade mansion remodelled for William Boyd of Keillers in 1921 by W. B. D. Keith (son of tenement Keith). Interior plasterwork particularly in the billiard room, and the glowing mahogany woodwork throughout the spacious hall and staircase is sumptuous. **THE LODGE** by the entrance, 47 Grove Road, is a delightful classical box, Ionic columns and a lunette above laughing where should have been a pediment. Vernon Constable, Thomsons assistant at the Caird Hall is said to have helped. In Fairfield Road,

104

mansions worth a glance include the eponymous **FAIRFIELD** c. 1868 which is the last survivor of Perth architect Andrew Heiton's houses; **INVERGARRY,** 10 Fairfield Road by Holt and Glover of Liverpool, 1903, and **RED COURT** (no. 17) 1885 by Hippolyte Blanc completed by G. G. MacLaren — a contrast to the rest of his high French roofs and confident Renaissance detailing in red stone. **INVERAVON,** originally Ethelstone, 2a Ellislea Road, once the home of D. C. Thomson, is another Italianate house by George Shaw Aitken, 1877, distinguished by its porch and wonderful conservatory. **MOYNESS,** 76 Grove Road is an 1876 Murray Robertson villa: there is little on the outside of stuccoed concrete to show whether the architect exploited the possibilities of the shuttered concrete he used.

On the corner of Strathern Road and Davidson Street, the rump of **BALLINARD,** enclosed within later hotel alterations rises proudly on its hill. Built by George Shaw Aitken for Watson of Watson's Bond in 1871 this vigorous Gothic house à la Owers retains its barge boarding, campaniles, and splendidly timber balconied west facade. Down on **DUNDEE ROAD,** in the grounds of **95** is the house James Parr built for himself in 1964, entered from the side to allow uninterrupted views to the sea. Downstairs, the hall takes the force of a central well, which can be merged with the dining room when required. The drawing room is upstairs, for the better view.

Number 26, **HARECRAIG** an 1835 villa extended in anchronistic 17th century Scots style by Mills and Shepherd 1905-7, adding the oriel and pyramid roof. In the grounds **THE ROCK** is a 1963 house cantilevered from the hillside by James Parr and Partners for a builder's son. The garden pool at the entrance extends into the house. **FORT WILLIAM,** 34 Dundee Road, the house of the Royal Tay Yacht Club is a curious Italianate 1839 villa in the style of George Mathewson, best seen from the shore: the central bay is a storey taller, with lower flanking bays, with a late regency flavour-enhanced by its Ionic loggia. **AYSTREE,** Victoria Road is a large, good quality mansion despite its half timbered gables by C. Ower and C. G. Soutar 1903. In **Beach Lane** there is a 1960s house by Professor James Paul.

Walker

above: The Royal Tay Yacht Club. *below:* 95 Dundee Road. *bottom:* The Rock.

Parr

Wishart

The Ferry. Colonel Hunter's house is bow-fronted, just above the castle.

BROUGHTY FERRY

Broughty Ferry is to Dundee what Southend was to London and Portobello is to Edinburgh: the nearest available seaside resort with the opportunity for some elite villas on Forthill and Barnhill above. Originally a fishing village around the castle-protected harbour called Partan Craig, it began to expand in the early nineteenth century, particularly after the improvement of roads and the arrival of the railway in 1848. About 1830, a chronicler noted that, *this village, of very late origin, is rapidly increasing. It owes its rise to having become a fashionable resort for sea bathing. The sea water here is very pure with a clean sloping beach. The village is built upon dry sand, which in some places is blown by the wind; and it admits of unlimited extension . . . Besides the resort for sea bathing, which only takes place during the summer, weavers and other mechanics are building houses and settling here.* In 1852, Lord Cockburn thought it *decidedly superior to Portobello. It is backed by a high rising ground . . . on which are perched an increasing variety of good gardened houses some of which are obviously excellent mansions; and it has a visible and near coast opposite instead of the boundless sea. But it wants the glorious Portobello sands . . . .*

The layout of the village between King and Queen Streets is based on a grid iron, devised by the feu superior Charles Hunter of Burnside in 1801, he who had himself erected **Broughty**

King Street

106

House, 97-99 Beach Crescent, on the edge of the harbour. A generally undistinguished house with red harling and a bow, it retains some pleasant internal features. It is thought that the construction of Colonel Hunter's own villa attracted others from the local squirearchy. A. J. Warden writing in 1888, commended the *enlightened foresight* of the architect who had provided such a clear layout and spacious streets. Unfortunately, the arrival of the railway vitiated much of the plan's success, dividing Broughty Ferry into two: the village down to the seashore; and the more select suburb Camphill with its *handsome villa residences each surrounded by enclosed gardens, with fine lawns, rich parterres and beautiful shrubberies; and many of them have spacious conservatories, vineries, etc,* all providing the *merchants, professional gentlemen and others whose business is in Dundee* with their slice of good life and echoes of Bournemouth.

The lower part of Broughty Ferry is dominated by:

19 **BROUGHTY CASTLE,** originally begun c. 1490. Completed by Andrew, second Lord Gray about 1496, Broughty Castle was of some strategic importance, governing a good harbour and the ferry point of Port-on-Craig, (thought to be Partan-Craig, or Crab Rock) which connected with Tayport. Its controller commanded the Tay. Consequently it was occupied by the English in 1547, during which time they erected a fort on Balgillo Hill, from which strangleholds they waged perpetual nuisance for the next two years. In 1550 the castle was recovered, but nine years later, the Protestant Scots faction took it once more, later to surrender it to the Catholics. As the Privy Council minute put it, *our auld ynemies of England being in the hous of Bruchty ar apperandly to invaid the burc of Dundie and haill cuntre, and to burn, herey, sla and destroy etc.* At that time the Castle consisted of a large square keep, with substantial outworks and high, fortified barmkin wall with towers at the corners.

After the troubles it clearly became the home of the Master of Gray prevented by his father from sharing Castle Huntly to the west. It does not seem to have been lived in after the mid-seventeenth century, but was still entire in 1716. In 1821 it was offered for sale, somewhat misleadingly on the basis that it could *be repaired at a small expense . . . and would make an excellent situation for an inn.* The restoration by R. Rowand Anderson for the

top: Fisher Street. *above:* Agnes Square.

War Office in 1861 was a virtual reconstruction: so much so that Warden refers to the *new castle having its attractions,* whereas the purists David MacGibbon and Thomas Ross ignore the new building entirely. Anderson's job was to provide a small military outpost to control the Tay. This he did by *restoring* the great square keep into an L-shaped one, partially harled, and by removing all traces of the outer buildings with their towers, replacing them with an interesting, inefficient mid-Victorian fortification. The Castle is now a museum open to the public: there is still a good harbour alongside; and Castle Green has a particularly well-equipped children's playground.

The shore in the 19th century, fishing boats drawn up on the shore.

The harbour is now used entirely for leisure; having once been the home of a fishing fleet, one of the first roll-on, roll-off ferries in Britain, and of a submarine mine unit of the Victorian volunteers. The Fisher Town of Broughty Ferry has that indefinable seaside atmosphere. Despite the grid-iron layout, there is the same sense of historic, small scale buildings huddling together against the elements, those in the major streets being aggrandised by Victorian commerce. **Brook** 110 **Street** opens with **ST STEPHEN'S CHURCH,** a 1871 cruciform church by T. S. Robertson with much good Morris and Co. glass inside.

At its eastern end, **ST AIDAN'S CHURCH,** 408 Brook Street, by James Black, 1824, is a prominent rubble church, whose square tower and slated spire overlooks the delightful **AGNES SQUARE** development of white houses designed in 1974 by James Parr and Partners. **PATTERSON'S SHOE SHOP** is identified by an elephantine, timber and bronzed glass representation of a boot; a nice 1977 conceit of *architecture parlante* by Robbie and Wellwood (Ric Russell). **KING STREET,** one south, is more lavish, the early shopfront at number 156, and the late eighteenth-century **Eagle Inn** 155-159 complete with James Law's 1860 eagle on the south wall deserving notice. The lovely classical house on the north-east corner with St Vincent Street, no. 150 King Street, is the best in the Ferry.

The shore line begins with **DOUGLAS TERRACE,** a pleasant series of ashlar semi-detached villas designed in 1838 by George Mathewson for himself; and continues with **1-13 JAMES PLACE,** a neo-classical terrace with chased stonework and curved corners, leading into **FISHER STREET,** the 1859 Negrétti and Zambia barometer i its stone case, (in no. 115), having proved its worth when the Ferry still had its fisher folk; and the 1973 housing association scheme at **BELLROCK SQUARE,** by James Parr and Partners, continuing a fishing aesthetic with harled walls, coloured window surrounds and a variegated roofscape. **BEACH CRESCENT** takes the shore round to General Hunter's villa, numbers 9-13 dating from c. 1800 and distinguished by a large fanlight to Gray Street, and by two classical villas, **Traquair** and **Beach House** (numbers 41-47). Number

top: The harbour today. *middle:* Patterson's shoe shop in the form of a glass boot. *above:* Fanlit doorway in Gray Street.

above: St Luke's, Broughty Ferry. *right:* The Library. *below:* The Eastern School.

Walker

Wishart

McKean

31 is the **ORCHAR ART GALLERY,** a larger than usual stone villa designed by J. Maclaren, 1866, for Stephens, the shipbuilder whose firm built Captain Scott's *Discovery,* vigorously extended to the rear by J. Findlay in 1936. Provost Orchar originally intended to have his gallery in a new building in Reres Park. He got as far as completing the 1897 gateway, but the endowment he left to house his splendid collection of nineteenth-century Scots paintings, comprising the largest collection of the nineteenth-century Scott-Lauder school of painting, was used to purchase an existing building instead.

The cross streets continue the engaging mixture of eighteenth- and nineteenth-century houses and cottages, in a variety of one and two storeys, some stone, some harled and some stucco; some slated, some tiled, with a collection of corbels, chimneys, doorcases, dormers, roofs and gables. **FORT STREET** is 116 best, beginning with **ST JAMES CHURCH** (number 5) 1889 by T. S. Robertson in the romanesque style; the **FISHERMAN'S TAVERN** (number 10) is a picturesque house: 32-34 being late eighteenth century with a good frieze, cornice and doorcase; 37-41 has a pilastered ground floor with an arcaded glazed corner with corbels and dormers above; 83-86 Fort Street, nearer the main commercial part of the town has original, florid 1885 shop fronts designed by H. J. Blanc, now altered. 117 **GRAY STREET** sports a great white boarded railway tower with florid cast iron, probably contemporary with the 1848 arrival of the railway redolent of the days when railways were exuberant and fun.

QUEEN STREET has become the main artery through the Ferry, notable for the churches with which it is dotted beginning, at the west, with H. J. Blanc's 1884 **ST LUKE'S** possibly the best church in the Ferry: a confident, red sandstone cruciform church, with good Morris and Co. glass in the apse. **ST MARY'S EPISCOPAL,** 164 Queen Street, is the inevitable Sir George Gilbert Scott, built from 1858 with a chancel lengthened by Sir Robert Lorimer in 1911. The *Ecclesiologist's* spy had no time to inspect: *a hasty glance from the railroad at the exterior does not enable us to say more than it seems a simple specimen of correct ecclesiology.* The former Queen Street Church, by George Shaw Aitken, 1876, is a well proportioned grouping of striped stone gables with tall western tower and protruding semi-hexagonal chancel to the east; facing onto the **LIBRARY,** a pleasant single-storey version of the Petit Trianon by James Maclellan Brown, the pilastered central bay projecting. At the corner of St Vincent Street the **BROUGHTY EAST CHURCH** is an early Gothic church by Andrew Heiton, 1865, with yet another unfinished tower. Just across the road, facing *Whinnybrae* is the **EASTERN SCHOOL,** a 1911 Langlands and Lamond Art Nouveau School in creamy stone, with the usual Mackintosh-esque lanterns on the roof, and large semi-circular windows in the gable.

Camphill Road was the ancient route to Monifieth, and has a number of good older buildings: **LOFTUS HOUSE,** No. 16 and **ST MARGARET'S,** No. 18, are both villas, the former with a bow front and Greek Ionic porch of 1835, the latter with a double-bow front subsequently Italianised, typical of the

Wishart

The view north used to be closed by the amazing fairy-tale skyline of **CASTLEROY,** 1867, designed by Andrew Heiton in a hard-edged neo-Tudor style, for the Gilroy dynasty; but it was demolished following an attack of dry rot, only its delightful Jacobean gatehouse closing Hill Street surviving. Down the hill at 7 Camphill Road was Castleroy's rival, **CARBET CASTLE (above),** of which the baronial gate lodge alone survives. The Grimonds camped here in an earlier house which they kept on extending in eccentric style as the size of the rival dynasty's palace became apparent. Dry rot, being even handed, did for the Grimonds as it had for the Gilroys.

above: The Bughties. *left:* 112 Camphill Road, by Gordon Allan. *bottom:* Strathmore Street.

Regency seaside. **CAMPHILL HOUSE** (no. 50) is an 1850 neo-Jacobean mansion in painted 122 stone by J. Maclaren, and the **BUGHTIES** nursing home (no. 76) an English-style 1882 mansion, rubble, half timbered, red tiles and brick chimneys showing the extent to which its architect J. Murray Robertson had been influenced by Richard Norman Shaw.

BARNHILL

Barnhill is an eastern suburb to Broughty Ferry, generally of pleasant, if later houses and lacking the sense of drama of the Ferry. Worthy of note, however, are **RERES HOUSE,** an 1849 barge-boarded, cottage mansion of the David Bryce type; a 1970's A-framed house by Gordon Allan; a 1974 housing scheme by Baxter Clark and Paul in **STRATHMORE STREET;** and private houses of the 1960's at nos. 2 and 6 Panmure Terrace. **FERNCROFT,** also Panmure Terrace, is a 1913 Thoms and Wilkie house, harled with stone margins. **LONGCROFT,** 2 Panmure Terrace, is a large 1922 house gone classical with loggia, hipped roof and Doric porch by Maclaren Soutar and Salmond; and Bonspiel Gardens, by Mercer Blaikie 1974, is an unobtrusive cul-de-sac of harled cottages. **2-4 INVERMARK TERRACE** have unusual stone details, and the 1895 St Margaret's across the road is yet another unfinished church, this time in Scots gothic, by Duncan Carmichael.

MONIFIETH

above: Ashludie. *below:* Grange House.
bottom: Tighnamuir.

Now seemingly an eastward extension of Broughty Ferry, but originally a village and parish in its own right — the one so brutally plundered by Auld Ballumbie in the 1570's (see pp.115). In 1845 it was described thus: *the village consists chiefly of thatched cottages, but has a somewhat extensive iron-foundry. In the burying ground surrounding the church — itself a plain but conspicuous building — are some beautifully carved antique tombstones, more tasteful and ornate than usually occur in rural cemeteries.* Like its neighbour, its glories lie in the hills looking south-east over the seas, and the villas which swarmed over them. Specific items of curiosity include the Gothic **ST RULES PARISH KIRK** (1813) by Samuel Bell without the proposed spire but making do with its little bell tower; the classically proportioned and detailed Manse by David Mackenzie (1829); the curious Grecian ornamentation lavished on the stucco cottage at 4 Hill Street; **GRANGE HOUSE** (1829), a small classical mansion by James Black, with sumptuous seventeenth-century Renaissance gate piers of caps, finials, mouldings and the like; the peculiar **BONE HOUSE** on The Laws, possibly put up in 1836 to contain the results of nearby excavations; and finally the plain belfried 1846 Monifieth **NORTH CHURCH.** Mansions of interest also include **ASHLUDIE,** large plain Jacobean by James Maclaren c. 1863; **TIGHNAMUIR** in red sandstone Jacobean by Murray Robertson; and **MILTON OF MONIFIETH,** an old mill house skilfully enlarged and remodelled by Thoms and Wilkie c. 1911.

Walker

Walker

H

OUTER DUNDEE AND HINTERLAND

This section deals with buildings and communities within a ten-mile radius of Dundee. It is divided into three sections, sharing the common inner boundary of Kingsway/Arbroath Road: east of Forfar Road, north between Forfar and Coupar Angus Roads, and west of the Coupar Angus Road. Individual buildings are either linked to self-contained communities or are listed chronologically. A common theme is the north-west — south-east route of the Dichty, whose riparian communities, dams, mills, bleachfields and viaducts are all part of the same pattern.

EAST OF FORFAR ROAD

Affleck

Ancient Monuments

[123] **AFFLECK OR AUCHINLECK CASTLE,** Monikie, late 15th century.

Ane old high tower house wrote the seventeenth-century writer Ochterlony *which is seen at a great distance at sea, and is used for a landmark by those that come in the river of the Tay.* It is one of the finest surviving tower houses in Scotland: complete, unpretentious and, difficult to visit. A beautiful L-shaped,

diagonally braced timber framing and metal lath. The bishop preferred brick but insisted on retaining the original elevations. The **KINGSWAY EAST FIRE STATION,** 1972, an elegantly geometric essay in single storey brickwork by James Parr and Partners; the large brilliant black-and-white mass of housing in **ALLOWAY TERRACE,** by Robbie and Wellwood 1976, like a stranded ocean liner, concealing its bulk well; the neighbouring student flats on Alloway Place West by Gauldie Wright and Partners 1983; the 1950's **ST VINCENT'S CATHOLIC CHURCH** and hall by W. W. Friskin; and **WHITFIELD CATHOLIC CHURCH,** 1973, by James Parr and Partners are all worthy of note.

Wishart

TEALING DOOCOT, Home Farm, dates from 1595, and is a fine rectangular crowstepped doocot with monogram DM and HG on the lintel, and moulded course to prevent vermin reaching the pigeons. There is much else of interest at Tealing: the **SOUTTERRAIN,** or underground earth house, dating from the Iron Age. Now roofless, this house has a passage, an 80-foot-long curved gallery, ending in a small chamber. It is an Ancient Monument accessible to visitors. The **PARISH CHURCH,** dates from 1806, whose inset stones include a tablet dated 1380, part of a medieval sacrament house and a high relief mural monument of 1618. The north gate of the kirkyard enclosure has a trefoil headed panel showing Christ in Glory; the **HEARSE HOUSE** (1806) has a crossbones inset stone; the recently renovated manse of 1803 is pleasantly symmetrical with a pilastered doorcase, with roughly contemporary stables and farm buildings — and a notable 1787 female sundial. **HILLSIDE OF PRIESTON** is the 1949 conversion of stone and slate cottage, byre and stable into a single house by the architect Arthur Wright for himself. **ST MARTIN'S STONE** at nearby Balkello Farm, is a fragment of a cross slab and shows relief carvings of a serpent and horseman.

Wishart

Walker

Ancient Monuments

Gauldie Wright

Conjectural reconstruction by David Walker of the courtyard of Mains Castle. *right:* The Castle today. The Flemish crow-stepped gables clearly visible.

McKean

131 **MAINS CASTLE, CAIRD PARK,** 1480-1700. The seat of the Grahams of Fintry since the sixteenth century, pleasantly set on a steep bank above a burn in the Dichty Valley, Mains — or Fintry — is a courtyard castle built progressively between 1480-1580. Its notable 70-foot-tall thin tower and adjacent hall block form the earliest parts of the castle now

surviving. The boldly carved main entrance is overshadowed by a projecting bartisan whose keystone is dated 1562, the initials DG and DMO standing for David Graham and Dame Margaret Ogilvy. The castle has a remarkable Renaissance stone panel with the motto in Latin: *grateful for country, for friends and for posterity.* The ground floor of the six-storey tower is a grand staircase with pleasant chambers above. The principal rooms were in the adjacent north wing, which contained a first floor hall, a private chamber and bedrooms above. The castle was abandoned as a residence after 1740, fell into ruin and is at last under reconstruction.

Baldovan House. The original entrance was up a flight of steps to the first floor level.

To the west, **OLD MAINS CHURCH,** 1800, with its bellcote and horse-shoe gallery stands in its own enclosure of stone walls and iron railings, an emblem of continuity in a district much transformed. It looks north, across the road, to **CLAVERHOUSE COTTAGES,** a somewhat neglected eighteenth-century village street. **CLAVERHOUSE, BLEACHFIELD OFFICES,** date from 1835-40, a two-storey building with bellcote. Claverhouse Bleachworks are the only survivors of the considerable number that used to exist on the Dichty.

BALDOVAN HOUSE, Old Glamis Road. Mid 18th century, new south frontal addition early nineteenth century. Large three-storey classical mansion seat of the Ogilvy family, (long involved in Dundee charitable projects,) through whose projecting central bay, designed as a triumphal arch, visitors entered directly into the piano-nobile at first-floor level. Front staircase later replaced by a porch. Service wing and stables on east by David Mackenzie 1831. Note also 1753 sundial.

STRATHMARTINE CASTLE, 1785. A small symmetrical Laird's mansion, with a double bow facing south, its *lang pedigree* evinced by two doocots: one about contemporary with pyramid roof (now ruined), the other a lean-to variety of the early seventeenth century. The Kirkton of Strathmartine has a pleasant 1791 twin-arched bridge with a toll house.

STRATHMARTINE PARISH CHURCH, 1843. Typical of the many churches built immediately after the Disruption, it is Norman in style with a wheel window added at the turn

An interesting contract survives for the construction of Baldovan Mill, on the Dichty, illuminating the simplicity of building in those days: it is between Dundee Council (client) and Andro Wast, Mason (builder) with the shadowy intervention of the Master Mason (architect) only in the location of the doors: January 1612: Town Council enter into contract with *Andro Wast, mason that he shall with all possible diligence build one sufficient mill house of stonework at Baldovan, of the length of fifty-two futts within the gables, and the breadth of twenty-two futts within the side walls, which shall be nine feet above the earth and the gables of height proportional. All the walls shall be of thickness two feet and a half foot, if they be built with lime; and if they be built with clay, three feet. Similarly, Andro shall build within the south side wall, in the most commodious place, ane great door of hewen stone of the wideness of twelve feet, and of the height of the side wall, having the towns arms well hewn above the same, with other two doors in such places as the Master of Work pleases design.*

of the present century by David Baxter. In the mid nineteenth century, the Ogilvys permitted the development of the **DOWNFIELD** and **BALDOVAN** suburbs linked by tram from and to the city centre, communities which were self contained and took pride in their identity. **BALDOVAN INDUSTRIAL SCHOOL,** Baldovan Road, James Maclaren, 1878, is a former approved school in stone Gothic with projecting wings, and a fine, central, Germanic spire, in a beautiful setting. **ST LUKE'S EPISCOPAL CHURCH,** Baldovan Road, Freeman and Ogilvy 1901 is a carefully designed homely church complex, with Scots details and stone dressings: otherwise white harled. So well done that at first glimpse it seems fifteenth or sixteenth century. On the edge of Kingsway itself is a small **GARDEN SUBURB** around Clive Road promoted by Sir Herbert Ogilvy in 1929, designed by the celebrated London architect W. Curtis Green (he of the Dorchester) and Sir Herbert's brother C. F. M. Ogilvy. It is a pleasant group of harled and slated houses, painted in shades of white and pink, with swept gables, dormer windows and traditional Scots details. **MAGDALENE KIRKTON** contains new houses in Ulverstone Terrace by the City Architect's Department, 1982, attracting attention by their bright pantiles, swept dormers, black timber work and coloured harling. The **NATIONAL CASH REGISTER** (Camperdown) building is a 1946 building by Beard and 134 Bennett of London; and the **TIMEX FACTORY,** a contemporary building by Beard and Bennett, is a long, low pink-brick building with projecting canopies and much of the sweep and style of the better 1930's buildings.

top: National Cash Register. *above:* Timex. *below:* Olivetti.

135 **OLIVETTI** factory by London architect Edward Cullian (1971) is a remarkable building whose first storey at the rear billows out over the lower, with a faintly Chinese effect caused by its triangular windows. On the other side, a largely glazed two-storey

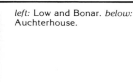

facade encloses three sides of a courtyard. The **LOW and BONAR** head office is a striking 1979 piece by Hugh Martin and Partners, a triangular, glass piano nobile projecting out over a square plinth.

AUCHTERHOUSE, mainly 17th century. Impressive ancient Scots mansion fashioned from a castle, part of the tower of which is embedded in the main building, the basement of another, "Wallace", tower lying to the south east. A stair tower, corbelled out as it rises in height, projects to the south. Some of the Jacobean plasterwork and fireplaces are as good as can be found in Scotland, probably dating from the time it came into the possession of James, Earl of Buchan, and possibly by the hand of Alexander White who worked at the Binns (West Lothian). Now an hotel.

In the village, **WHITETOPS** (1967 c.) Baxter Clark and Paul (James Paul) is certainly unusual; a fruit salad of large monopitched roofs, splayed rough cast walls, and spacious interior (formerly with inside water garden).

The old **PARISH KIRK** and Kirkyard is of particular quality, being a 1630 construction upon a medieval foundation, retaining fifteenth-century chancel arch and doorway. The clock dates from 1740.

AUCHTERHOUSE Kirk Session, having saved to install glass windows in the seventeenth century, experienced a wanton woman falling asleep in the kirkyard outside during communion who, resting her head against the new glazing, went right through it.

right: The original drawing for Kinpurnie Castle. *above:* Some clear differences as built in the entrance porch, the central gable and the dormer storey. *below:* The 1833 Newtyle railway engine constructed by Carmichael's of Dundee.

140 **NEWTYLE** to the west, has two items of specific note: **KINPURNIE CASTLE** an informal, seventeenth-century style (1911) house, by Thoms and Wilkie, whose entrance is between two turreted drum towers, white harled, the rest being in mid seventeenth-century Scots to suit: and the **RAILWAY STATION,** a relic of the 1831 Dundee-Newtyle railway on which the trains had to be hauled by stationary steam engines up the inclines at each end, the locomotive only operating on the flat. From time to time, the company also used sails and horses.

The Parish Church with its tall gabled tower, was designed by Andrew Heiton in 1872. Nearby **BANNATYNE HOUSE,** home of George Bannatyne the collector of old Scots poetry, is a seventeenth-century house Victorianised by Leslie Ower, but still retaining an angle turret and its white harling. **HATTON CASTLE,** nearby, is a large L-plan castle built in 1575, the main entrance and staircase of which was in the west wing leading up to a spacious first floor hall. A much smaller circular staircase in the re-entrant of the east wing linked the hall to the kitchen and larder below.

above: Camperdown House

OUTER WEST DUNDEE

CAMPERDOWN HOUSE
William Burn, 1824.
Erected by the son of one of Dundee's most famous products, Admiral Duncan, Viscount Camperdown, titled after the victory he scored over the Dutch, this stately home with its magnificent park is one of Dundee's glories, although its use would not reflect that. It is a neo-classical mansion similar to William Wilkins' famous Grange in Hampshire: its portico occupying the entire eastern, ie narrow, facade, allowing the long, plainly modelled and pilastered south front unobstructed enjoyment of the view over the gardens and river. It also allowed an uninterrupted sequence of state rooms along the south front. The design is clearly derivative of Burn's 1812 scheme for Dalmeny House for the Earl of Rosebery, and the house is in the very highest rank of Scottish country houses. The glory of the interior is the double height hall, roofed and lit by a stained glass dome surmounted on semi eliptical pendentives.

Just above the house in **TEMPLETON WOODS** is a smart, angular new Ranger Centre by Jack Fulton, under the aegis of the City Architect, with a jewel-like clarity of triangular form. It was built with MSC labour.

The **DUNCAN MAUSOLEUM,** in Lundie Kirkyard five miles away, was designed by Robert Mylne in 1789. It occupies the site of the chancel of the old Kirk, Georgianised medieval but mostly restored by T. S. Robertson in 1892. The nearby manse dates

Camperdown is odd in that the Lord and lady had their living quarters in a single storey extension to the north, and the rooms are so planned that Lady Camperdown could have free use of the house without ever meeing either guest or servant.

Templeton Woods Ranger Centre

Wishart

from 1797, and the Beadle's House is Tudor Gothic.

143   Back on the by-pass, **NATIONAL CASH REGISTER'S** offices, by Wylie Shanks and Underwood, 1949, and the 1946 Beard and Bennett first (Camperdown) building have immense dignity: simple, well-detailed proportion, brick, thin concrete frames and glass compensating for their plainness.

LIFF
144 A hillside village of pleasant aspect now swamped by Dundonian exiles. Note

Liff Church

Walker

particularly the 1839 **PARISH KIRK** — gothic with a self-important spire, by William Mackenzie, sitting very neat and proper in its well-groomed Kirkyard; note also the Gothic Hearse House, and the classically columned nineteenth-century Webster Monument (now minus its urn), the nearby mill (rebuilt 1865); and **Red Roofs,** Loch of Liff Road — possibly eighteenth-century *fermtoun* building of house and byre: interesting for its clay walls and corrugated iron roof: and an example of the genuine rural vernacular of the district. The **Lunatic Asylum** 1874, (now Royal Dundee (Liff) Hospital) is a huge symmetrical baronial building by Edward and Robertson, now much diminished in interest; and the adjacent Gowrie House by T. S. Robertson 1901.

FOWLIS EASTER

left: Details of Fowlis Collegiate Church drawn in 1855. *above:* The Sacrament House, measured by W. F. Howitt.

A small hillside community, containing perhaps Scotland's finest surviving small medieval **CHURCH,** still retaining all the decorative joy the Reformers extirpated elsewhere — part of its fine rood screen, medieval paintings, alms dish, sacrament house and font. Good plain Gothic traceried windows. Lord Gray had tried, unsuccessfully, to establish a collegiate church at Fowlis in the mid fifteenth century, from which attempt its surviving glories probably date. A second attempt to achieve full collegiate status in 1538 was successful. Other items of interest in this hillside village are: the pre reformation cross; **FOWLIS CASTLE** (1640 with 1840 wing) a particularly unmilitary three-storey tower house with projecting turreted stair; the 1841 Hearse House; plain 1855 Schoolmaster's House, with a pleasing symmetry and projecting central bay; picturesque eighteenth-century Waulkmill Bridge. The castle is of particular interest, being the sole remnant of a much larger courtyard castle.

Above: Fowlis Castle

THE powerful House of Gray whose original seat Fowlis was, also built both Broughty Castle and Castle Huntly, and indirectly Invergowrie house. The Grays always moved on, from Fowlis to Huntly, Huntly to House of Gray and, in the nineteenth century, from House of Gray to Kinfauns Castle. The most famous member of the family connected with Fowlis was the Master of Gray, who was banished for the crime of procuring the death of Mary Queen of Scots in England whilst employed to intercede on her behalf; an accusation subsequently shown to be largely erroneous.

147 **GRAYBURN,** Benvie Road, is a rural Arts and Crafts retreat nestling behind rubble walls under long swooping slate roofs, low slung eaves. It was designed in 1905 by architect Patrick Thoms for his uncle. **BENVIE FARMHOUSE,** across the road, is a beautiful, early eighteenth-century structure, almost entirely rebuilt after fire in the early twentieth century.

below: Grayburn. *below left:* Benvie Farmhouse.

6 HOUSE OF GRAY,
1716, Alex McGill and John Strachan
Built by the 12th Lord Gray, the House is a
very fine Scots essay, with symmetrical north
and south facades. It consists of central block
with pedimented centre bay and flanked by
ogee-capped stairtowers, and wings on either
side. It is not classical in the sense that William
Adam's Somerville House is a classical: rather
it is the apotheosis of the native Scots country
house: not unlike a miniature version of Sir
William Bruce's house of Nairne or the larger
original Mount Stuart in Bute. The continuing
uncertainty over this fine house has been a
scandal. Happily, restoration is about to be
begun anew.

above: Invergowrie about 1900. below: A carved stone in the old church.

Dundee District Libraries

Odd village. That perceived from the main road is but the tip of the iceberg, the remainder of which straggles in copious but diffuse quantities down to the shore and the station, including ranks of plain white 1930's semi-detached. The antiquity of the place is not in doubt. It figures in **Wynton's Oryginal Chronikall** and the remains of St Peter's (or Dargie) Kirk, possibly sixteenth century, down by the shore is the evidence of such antiquity; so, also, used to be (before they were buried in the land reclamation 'twixt railway and road) two ancient stones called the Goors of Gowrie, of which Thomas the Rhymer is reputed to have uttered:

When the Goors of Gowrie come to land
The Day of Judgement is at hand:

It wasn't. The village became a company village with the success of the Bullionfield Paper Mill whose castellated relic lies by the burn to the north. On the very shore itself is **TAYSIDE,** a 1952 conversion of stone cottages for Kingoodie quarrymen into a smart riverside house on two levels, by Gauldie Hardie Wright and Needham. The **PARISH CHURCH,** by John Robertson, was built with money from Lady Armitstead as a riposte to Lady Kinnaird's patronage of All Souls; in an almost decoration-free chunky Gothic displaying the stonemason's craft to good effect. **GREYSTANE,** now the Swallow Hotel, is an 1870 testimony to the ambitions of Bullionfield's owner. Designed by Campbell Douglas it is a tall, baronial tower house with excellent plaster and timber work. Buildings of interest on the main road are the **Toll House** — pleasant, single storey, harled house with prominent projecting bow; the 1849 **Manse** — a harled building with stone margins with a pedimented doorway; the 1844 former **Free Church** (now Bullionfield Recreation Club) — a rectangular box with Romanesque tower and addition (1906) by Thoms and Wilkie; and the aggressive **All Souls Episcopal** in confident and bullish red stone, 1891, by Hippolyte Blanc, inside which you will find a stone pulpit, marble reredos, and a chancel rib-vaulted in timber. **THE GOWS,** is a good mansion with a Frenchified roofscape by Charles Kinnear of Peddie and Kinnear 1864.

The most important building, however, is historic **INVERGOWRIE HOUSE**, in the lee of Ninewells Hospital. What can be seen today dates from 1600 greatly reconditioned and

above: Greystane, now Swallow Hotel.

There is a bump at the bottom of Invergowrie Park variously attributed to a medieval motte, and to the location of a telescope belonging to an eighteenth-century salt who liked to keep an eye on the Firth (or maybe radicals approaching from Dundee). In reality, it is an icehouse.

altered in 1837 by William Burn. However parts of each wing could predate 1600, to a medieval L-shaped tower. Patrick Gray extended the old building in 1600 providing a new staircase tower and dormer windows carrying his initials and those of Anne Napier, his wife, ending up with a typical seventeenth-century U-plan home with corner stair towers.

above: Invergowrie House.
below: Tayside.

KINGOODIE. Just west of Invergowrie was a mining and quarrying village, the stone from its quarries being celebrated for sea wall and harbour work although the quarries were no longer worked after 1895. **Linlithgow Place**, of the 1920's, is an excellent pair of Scots stone and slate, well-detailed houses for quarry workers, by Patrick Thoms.

LONGFORGAN

Beautiful village to the west of Dundee, mercifully rescued by the by-pass. It consists mostly of whitewashed single storey eighteenth-century cottages with appropriate honeysuckle and clambering foliage with some later Victorian stone villas. Specific

McKean

items of interest are: **PARISH KIRK,** a plainly elegant rubble box kirk of 1794, enhanced by picturesque 1690 tower symmetrically placed against the west gable, a tiny stone spire protruding through the tower's balustrade. Interior bombed out by Alexander Hutcheson, 1900, in the interests of the ecclesiological refurnishing. Later screens by Sir Robert Lorimer. Note also, **School House,** John Bell 1833, with its stone Tudor Gothic details and porch, **THE ELMS,** Main Street, by Thoms and Wilkie, 1910, recognisable by its stone, its eaves, the tiny central window and its dormers; a modern brick extension to the bowling club; and the new pantiled house terminating the village at its east end. The **Manse** is a large two-storeyed building with a shallow bow, designed by David Neave in 1823. **THE CROFT,** by Murray Robertson, 1895, is a villa of considerable charm with large chimneys, diamond-paned glass and receding roofs on each storey, cottage style.

Walker

left: The Croft.

52 CASTLE HUNTLY,
1452 onwards.

Built by the Barons Gray to replace their existing castle at Fowlis, Castle Huntly is clasped to a rock that surges out of what was once the floodplain of the Tay and is now, in no small measure due to its eighteenth-century proprietor George Paterson, the rich fields and orchards of the Carse of Gowrie. Originally a large L-plan towerhouse with vaulted lower storeys, it was extensively altered when, having been purchased by the Lyon family, Patrick, Earl of Strathmore became the occupier in 1647. His account of the castle and alterations is preserved at Glamis Castle. It was extended again in the eighteenth and nineteenth centuries, and has now been expropriated by the Scottish Home and Health Department for use as a Borstal which, it seems, generates the same pride and *esprit de corps* in its inmates as that allegedly apparent in public schools. The **North Gate** of the castle is a remarkable seventeenth-century composition, rebuilt here in 1783. The gate piers are square, with attached classical columns, topped with stone spires like those at Moray House in Edinburgh, flanked on either side by curvilinear enclosing walls.

In 1684 Earl Patrick recorded how he found the castle upon inheritance, and what he did with it. *My grandfather made this purchase from the Lord Gray at which time save that the land was speciall good it was a place of no consideratione, fit for nothing else but a place of refuge in time of trouble wherein a man might make himself a prisoner . . . I wish that everie man that has such houses would reform them; for who can delight to live in a house as in a prisone . . . My father . . . put on an inteer new roofe upon the Castle and Jamm which before had ane old scurvie battlement . . . The house stands upon a verie stubborne rock . . . all the levellings when done so under cover disguise that its scarce to be beleeved what work or labour there has been at the doing of it . . . The house itself was extremly cold and the hall was a vault of of which . . . I have gained the rooms immediately above it: no access there was to the upper part of the house without going through the hall even upon the most undecent occasions of drudgery . . . There were three new windows shaped out and made in the storie of the low hall, and a back stair upon it, another back stair from the vestibule of the high dining room to the very top . . . all digged out of the thickness of the wall, seven closets out of the wall, the new rooms gained out of the deepness and height of the vault of the old hall . . . and the bed chamber above the drawing room reformed with new light to the south.*

DUNDEE ACROSS THE WATER

Tayport, Newport and Wormit have a special relationship with Dundee.

WORMIT

at the southern edge of the Tay Railway bridge, became celebrated as the last contact with the 5.27 p.m. train from Burntisland on 28th December 1879 which was lost with all passengers as the High Girders at the centre of the bridge were blown over in the storm. It owed its existence to the railway which put it within easy commuter distance of Dundee and consists of primarily late Victorian villas in rows up and down the hillside. There are two

Sandford House Hotel *(right)*.

Wishart

¹⁵⁴ buildings of interest. **SANDFORD HOUSE,** (hotel), one of only two works in Scotland by the celebrated English Arts and Crafts architect Mackay Hugh Baillie Scott (1913) with much sweeping of steep roof, harling and highly crafted timberwork. It has been admirably extended by Robert Hurd and Partners. **23 NAUGHTON ROAD** is an 1888 single-storey, symmetrical villa between whose bay windows there is a five-bay loggia on cast iron columns. Riverside Road leads to Woodhaven, originally the principal ferry point for Dundee. **WOODHAVEN FARMHOUSE,** 92 Riverside Road, is an 1820, classical, former Inn.

NEWPORT
ON TAY

West Road leads into Newport: again, a relatively modern community whose origins — apart from the tiny community of salmon fishermen who always survived on the south bank — go little further back than the start of the nineteenth century when the lairds of Tayfield provided a harbour principally used for the export of produce. The reorganisation of Dundee's harbour and ferry, and the introduction of the steam ferries, led to the discontinuation of the Woodhaven ferry service in 1822 and the erection of a new Ferry terminal at the bottom of Boat Brae. The effect on Newport was dramatic, for it provided another bolt hole in which industrialists from Dundee could live clear of their effluent, and another opportunity for ordinary Dundonians to take jaunts on the **Fifie** across the water. By 1844, *some way both east and west of Newport a number of elegant marine villas have been erected which, with their gardens and shrubberies, add greatly to the interest of this portion of the landscape . . . chiefly erected by merchants and others belonging to Dundee for the benefit of the sea bathing during the summer.* By 1873, the *many elegant private residences built in terraces on the slopes which rise up from the river* attracted notice; *not a few professional and business*

top: The view to Dundee from Newport.
above: Trinity Church.

above: The Terrace.

men have taken up their permanent abode here. The Burgh is linear in plan following the contours of the steep, north-facing cliff of the Tay.

Along West Road one might notice number
155 **94,** an 1840, classical house with a good fanlight and unusual doorway; **THE CASTLE,** (53-59) a harled row with slim circular towers crenellated at the top, and trellis balconies at first floor. **70 WEST ROAD** is a nice classical cottage in rusticated ashlar, with an Ionic columned porch; **58-28 WEST ROAD** provides a fine group of early nineteenth-century buildings including Heathfield House, the Strawberry-Hill mock gothic Castle Cottage, the Jacobean Rockcliffe, the Italian-towered Broadhaugh (1828); and the **TERRACE,** (28-42) a picturesque and idyllic 1840 row of vaguely Tudor alms houses, with blank dormer gables, fanlit doors and ranks of chimneys. **BALMORE** and **WESTWOOD** are both large 1860's villas with lodge houses, both Italianate and both towered, Westwood being designed by Andrew Heiton. **NEWPORT**
156 **HOTEL** is an 1806 former coaching inn with a classical facade. The splendidly sited **TRINITY CHURCH** on the opposite corner is a curiosity of 1881 by C. & L. Ower, its octagonal tower forming a landmark, beckoning down to the now disused pier. Boat Road now looks rather sad and neglected and the 1930's modern block of shops and cafes would benefit from whitewash. The Italianate Ferry building (C. & L. Ower again), with their extravagant columns looks very smart. On the hill above are the policies of **TAYFIELD HOUSE,** a Tudor-styled remodelling of an older building by George Smith, 1828, the two estate lodges being

contemporary and in keeping. **ABERCRAIG,** (2 West Road), Tayfield's dower house, dates from 1840 and has a semi-circular Doric porch. Single-storey to the road, its canted bay front to the river extends down the cliff face.

Central Newport consists of many fine villas and terraces uphill. The terrace at **CUPAR ROAD** is a range of Egyptian-looking stone gate posts, good doorways and twinned chimney stacks corbelled out above a datestone. 61 Cupar Road, opposite, is a corner villa with Dutch gable, half-timbered porch and ogee-capped bay of the Murray Robertson school of design. Downhill, the **RIO CINEMA,** now a youth club, is a good 1930's exercise in disguise, being the conversion of an older building. Modernity arrives in Newport down a lane (so it offends no one) and consists of two heavily projecting cornices punctuated at the corner by three lumpy fins the central one curving up to the roof in a distant echo of the Grosvenor, Rayner's Lane, London. **ST MARY'S EPISCOPAL CHURCH** is a Gothic 1886 building by T. M. Cappon with a bellcote. **60-64 TAY STREET** form an excellent pair of Italianate semi-detached houses with broad eaves, the single-storey north-facing wings being occupied by Venetian windows, 48 Tay Street is a former coaching inn, also contemporary, with fanlight and wallhead gable; number **56** is Tudor from 1860, projecting gables, crenellated bays and a good wooden porch between; number **8-10** is a classically designed 1840 building with key stones. On the other side of the road, **SEYMOUR HOUSE HOTEL** is vigorous red sandstone Dutch.

top: The Ferry buildings. *above right:* The Rio Cinema. *right:* 60-64 Tay Street.

K

TAYPORT

The railway company was responsible for the name Tayport: the community's historic title, and that of the parish, is Ferryport-on-Craig, suitably similar to its twin on the northern shore, Partan-Craig (or Broughty Ferry). The village is historic, and Castle Street commemorates a now vanished fortification; although it is now predominantly mid-nineteenth century in character, with good stone-built villas and terraces laid out on a grid-iron down the slope. Some pantiled or slated harled fisherman's cottages still survive down toward the shore, particularly in **WHITEHILL** (numbers 1, 14, 16, 18, 20, 22 and 24); in Butter Wynd, School Wynd and Rose Street. The **PARISH CHURCH** of 1794 and 1825 is set snug into the hill above the sea, its square leaning stone clock tower rising centrally in the sea facade, from above the Scotscraig vault. Armorial stones in the tower, and gravestones in the Kirkyard date from the seventeenth century. **THE OLD PARISH MANSE,** 10 Maitland Street, is a larger, whitewashed rubble house. In its current form, Tayport harbour dates from 1847, constructed by the Edinburgh and Northern Railway. **PILE LIGHTHOUSE,** out to sea is a superstructure on stilts dating from 1848-49 possibly designed by Dundee's Harbour engineer Charles Ower. **TAYPORT PRIMARY SCHOOL,** 1875, is a fairly good Gothic building with pinnacles, a sign of the Burgh's growing wealth. Down on the Shore, there is a large block of 1930's flats by the harbour, and pleasant modern harled cottages in President Grant Place. On **WEST COMMON,** the 1832 East Lighthouse, complete with balcony and octagonal cupola, came from the hand of Robert Stevenson, grandfather of Robert

below: Castle Street, named after a gigantic Z-plan castle whose foundations survived to the 19th century. *far right:* New houses by North East Fife District Council down by the shore. *middle right:* The parish church. *bottom right:* St Mary Star of the Sea.

Wishart

159

138

Louis; the adjacent **1 West Lights** is a simple lightkeepers cottage of the same date. **TAYSIDE HOUSE** is an 1820 cottage with original door, fanlight and knocker, whilst the **West Lighthouse** and **7 and 8 West Lights** are again by Stevenson, same age and date as East Lights. **INN STREET** boasts Inn Cottage (now Manana, but formerly the Scotscraig Inn), a large 1800 house with a stone vaulted ice-house; and eighteenth century, pantiled, whitewashed, Harbour Cottages. In **ALBERT STREET,** note 7-31 Isla Place, late Victorian, harled brick houses for Tay Bridge workers,

Wishart

Wishart

and 1827 **Argyle House** with it pilastered doorway. **GREENSIDE PLACE** is of interest, number 8 being eighteenth century, 4-6 early nineteenth and two being late Victorian. **THE COTTAGE,** 2 William Street, is a pleasant, single-storey regency house of 1810, whilst number 36 William Street is early nineteenth century with rusticated stonework and Doric columns. **ST MARY STAR OF THE SEA,** at the eastern entrance to the burgh, is a shining bright Scots church designed by Reginald Fairlie, 1939, with octagonal tower, gothic details and sculptures by Hew Lorimer

Wishart

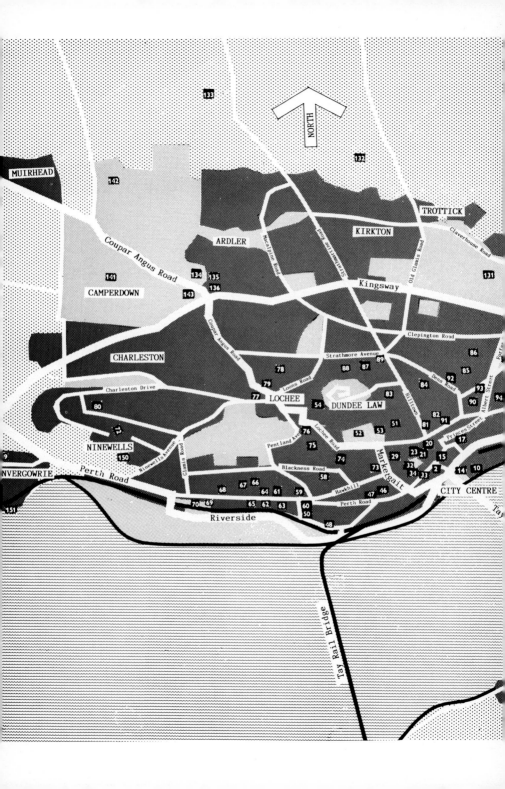

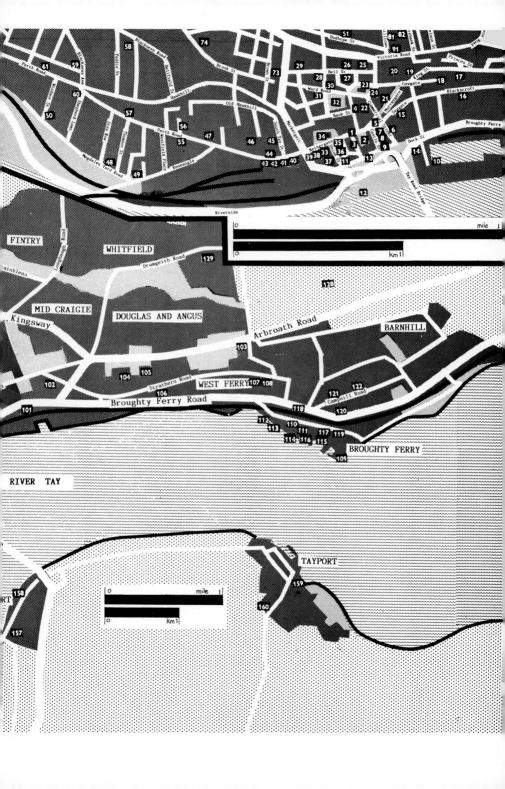

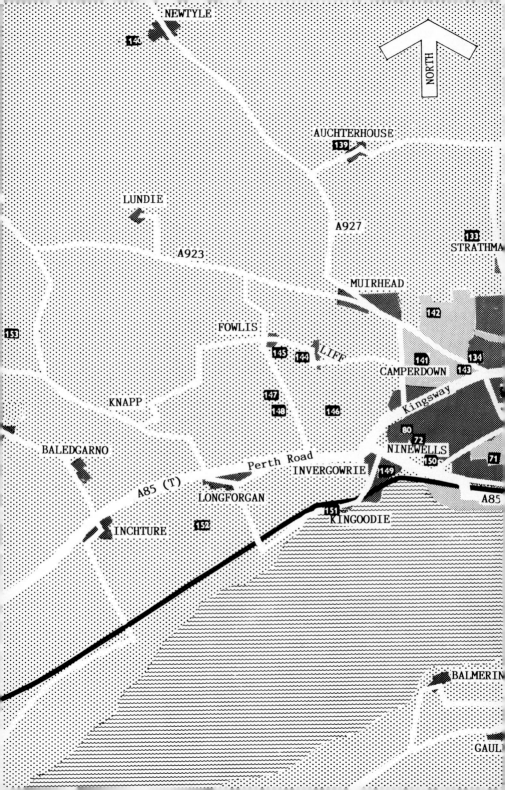

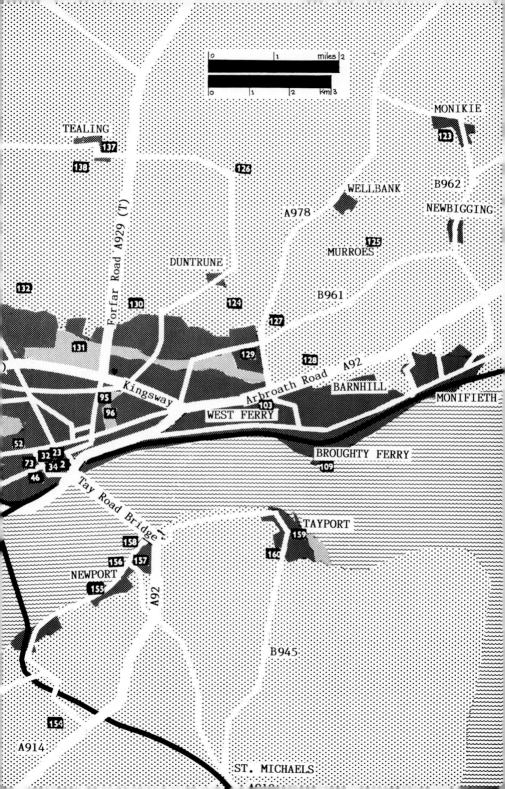

ACKNOWLEDGEMENTS

The authors and publishers are indebted to many people and organisations who have provided help, support, and encouragement. First, the Landmark Trust provided a gift to the Royal Incorporation in recognition of the RIAS' involvement with The Hill House, Helensburgh; the gift's purpose being to facilitate the publication of architectural books in Scotland. Further, this book could not have been published without the agreement to pre-purchase by the City of Dundee District Council and the Scottish Development Agency.

Particular thanks are due to Sinclair Gauldie, PPRIAS, Enid Gauldie, Thomas H. Thoms, PPRIAS, Colin Wishart, the appointed representative of the Dundee Institute of Architects, and Professor Alan Lendrum, all of whom were kind enough to contribute detailed knowledge and advice.

Comments and advice were also received from Andrew Nicoll, President of the Dundee Institute of Architects, Angus MacDonald, Senior Vice-President, Arthur Wright, PPRIAS, Michael Merchant, Ian Gow, Miss Catherine Cruft, Roland Paxton, Anne Riches, Richard Emerson, David Wishart, Ian Platt, Robert Dron, Ian Stout, Jeff Lonsdale, John Yellowlees, Geoffrey Stell, John Clark, and Dick Dewar. Paul Clark's thesis on Thoms & Wilkie was of particular interest. Staff of the Dundee District Libraries, particularly Mr Kett, were most helpful and provided us with illustrations not before seen, as did the Buildings Office of the University of Dundee. Thanks are also due to the SDD Ancient Monuments Division, and to Alan Peden.

A large number of people have contributed to the 280 photographs in this volume: Colin Wishart took the majority, followed closely by Stanley P. Turner, formerly of the University of Dundee; and the photographic collection of the University Library. Dundee District Public Libraries, and the National Monuments Record provided copious illustrations, the latter giving access to all the surviving Dean of Guild drawings. J. J. Herd of the North British Traction Group was also helpful. Maps were prepared by David MacDougall and Alan Rodgers, the design is by James Forbes and Charles McKean; and the production by John McWilliam and Charles McKean.

REFERENCES

A large number of books have been consulted in the preparation of this volume, including the excellent handbooks by the Abertay Historical Society — particularly *Architecture and Architects in Dundee, Mains Castle and the Grahams of Fintry, Broughty Castle. Dundee Textile Industry 1790-1885* (the papers of Peter Carmichael) edited by Enid Gauldie was of particular help, as were the Handbooks of the British Association's visits to Dundee in 1912-1968; the publications by Messrs William Kidd in the late 19th century; *Dundee Celebrities* by William Norrie; the *Builder;* the *Ecclesiologist,* the *Baronial and Ecclesiastical Antiquities of Scotland* by Robert Billings; *Theatrum Scotia* by Captain John Slezer; the *History of Dundee* edited by James Maclaren; and the *Castellated and Domestic Architecture of Scotland* by David MacGibbon and Thomas Ross. Thanks are due to the Libraries of the Royal Incorporation of Architects in Scotland and the Edinburgh Architectural Associaion for permission to reproduce from and to consult their volumes.

The photograph on the cover of this volume was taken by Eric Blair, and the sources of the remaining illustrations are as follows:
Colin Wishart, 4, 5, 6, 16, 18, 19, 28, 30, 31, 33, 34, 35, 38, 41, 54, 55, 56, 57, 58, 59, 64, 76, 77, 79, 81, 84, 85, 88, 89, 90, 91, 93, 96, 98, 99, 100, 103, 104, 105, 106, 107, 109, 110, 111, 117, 118, 119, 122, 124, 125, 131, 134, 138, 139. Charles McKean, 8, 15, 17, 26, 27, 47, 48, 49, 50, 51, 60, 65, 66, 68, 72, 73, 75, 76, 78, 82, 84, 86, 87, 101, 109, 110, 120, 128, 131, 132, 133, 135, 136, 137. The Royal Commission on the Ancient and Historical Monuments, Scotland, 12, 14, 16, 18, 21, 22, 23, 24, 38, 39, 40, 42, 46, 54, 66, 70, 76, 81, 87, 92, 95, 112, 115, 123, 127, 129, 135. Dundee District Public Libraries, 11, 13, 15, 17, 18, 20, 21, 43, 52, 53, 73, 75, 77, 78, 130. RIAS Library, 16, 19, 34, 43, 44, 49, 90, 91, 96, 97, 124, 127. Richard Davies, 20, 32, 43, 62, 66, 95. Dundee District Council, 29, 40, 50, 94, 101. David Walker, 14, 26, 45, 46, 55, 80, 81, 97, 98, 105, 106, 108, 110, 111, 113, 116, 119, 121, 126, 128, 132. University of Dundee, 2, 7, 9, 10, 30, 63, 65, 82, 124. Baxter Clark & Paul, 29, 46, 67, 112. Nicoll Russell Studio, 62, 104, 109. France

Smoor, 116. Stanley Turner, 18, 25, 63, 64, 68, 69, 83, 130. James Parr, 36, 67, 86, 105, 107. Gauldie Wright, 39, 119, 131. PSA 48, 71, 103. Spanphoto, 65, 83. Alan Rodgers, 74. Thoms and Nairn, 80, 81, 82, 103. Alan Peden, 93. SDD Ancient Monuments, 102, 114, 119. Gordon Allen, 112. Hugh Martin, 123.

James Thomson's unexecuted design for a new Civic Centre on the Earl Grey Dock.

Architects working in Dundee

A

Adam, William (1689-1748), 10, 14

Aitken, George Shaw (1836-1921: app. John Dick Peddie 1850: partner James Maclaren 1873-1877: on his own 1878-1881, thereafter Edinburgh,) 16, 19, 77, 104, 105, 111

Alexander, William (1841-1904: app. James Maclaren, c. 1855: commenced practice Dundee, 1865), 40, 48, 75, 96

Allan, William (d. 1945: app. Maclaren Soutar Salmond: commenced practice Dundee, 1919),

Allen, Gordon, 112

Anderson, J. F. (assistant to Robert Keith and others, Dundee)

Anderson, Sir R. Rowand & Paul (1834-1921: app. John Lessels; dr. Lt. Col. Moody R.E. and Sir G. G. Scott, commenced practice Edinburgh, c. 1862), 65, 107-8

Anderson, William James (c. 1863-1900: app. J. Gillespie, St Andrews: dr. Anderson & Browne; to T. L. Watson: commenced practice Glasgow, 1889), 15

Angus, George (1792-1845: app. dr. William Burn: commenced practice Edinburgh, 1825), 47, 48, 75

Arkos Design, 82

Armour, Charles, 28

B

Baillie, Scott M. H., 134

Barlow, W. H., 70

Baxter, David W. (d. 1957: app. Alexander Johnston & J. M. Robertson: in partnership with Johnston c. 1896), 16, 28, 49, 82, 90, 96, 99

Baxter Clark & Paul, 46, 67, 112, 123

Beard and Bennett, 122

Bell & Farquharson, 77

Bell, Samuel (1739-1813: app. father John Bell, Wright, Dundee), 13, 22, 35, 52-3, 58-9, 60, 62, 113

Bissett, C. J., 28

Black, James (d. 1841: commenced practice 1805, came to Dundee 1817), 3, 48, 75, 109, 113

Blaikie, Mercer, 112

Blanc, Hippolyte Jean (1844-1921: app. D. Rhind: dr. R. Matheson: commenced independent practice Edinburgh, c. 1872), 105, 110, 111, 131

Bodley, George Frederick (1827-1907: app. Sir G. G. Scott, commenced practice London, 1860), 93

Boswell, George A. (c. 1880-1952: commenced practice Glasgow, c. 1907), 39

Bouch, Sir Thomas, 69

Brewster, James (c. 1805-1845: came to Dundee from Montrose, 1832), 49

Brown, J. MacLellan, 15, 96, 111, 118

Browne, Sir George Washington (1853-1939: app. James Sellars: dr. J. J. Stevenson, Sir Arthur Blomfield, W. E. Nesfield, R. R. Anderson: partner Anderson, Edinburgh 1881-1885, independent practice Edinburgh, 1885), 21

Bruce, John, & Sons (commenced practice Dundee and Carnoustie, c. 1870)

Bryce, David (1803-1876: app. William Burn, later dr. and Edinburgh partner 1841-1850), 43, 44-5

Burke, Ian, Martin & Partners, 15

Burn, William (1789-1870: app. Robert Burn and Sir Robert Smirke: commenced practice Edinburgh, 1812. After 1844, London), 16, 52, 54, 115, 125, 131

Burnet, Sir John James (1857-1938: app. John Burnet Sen.: École des Beaux Arts, atelier Jean Louis Pascal; dr. Francois Rolland: returned to father, Glasgow, c. 1877, after 1904 London and Glasgow), 15

Butterfield, William (1814-1900: pupil E. L. Blackburne, 1833-1836: dr. Inwoods: commenced practice London)

C

Cappon, Thomas Martin (d. 1939: app. C. & L. Ower: commenced practice c. 1889), 34, 64, 92, 96, 137

Carmichael, C. C. (Aberdeen) and Duncan (London)

Carmichael, Peter (1809-1891: engineering partner, Baxter Brothers), 30, 31, 34

Chalmers, William (1829-? commenced practice Broughty Ferry, c. 1860), 101

Clunas, David, 93

Coe, Henry Edward (Coe & Goodwin) 1825/6-1885: app. Sir G. G. Scott: commenced practice London, c. 1850, 74, 86

Cousin, David (1809-1878: app. and dr. W. H. Playfair: commenced practice Edinburgh, c. 1838)

Cox, George Addison (1821-1899: engineer partner, Cox Brothers), 88-9

Cullinan, Edward, 122

D

Douglas, Campbell, 131

Dundee District Council Architects, 77, 92, 95, 96, 100, 122, 125

E

East, Harry (dr. T. M. Cappon: emigrated to Canada 1897, died soon afterwards)

Edward, Charles (of Edward and Robertson 1816-1890: trained as builder: commenced practice, Dundee, c. 1850), 32, 49, 75, 96, 104, 126

Elliot, Randolph (mill engineers, Glasgow)

Ellis, Alexander (1836-1917: app. William Smith, c. 1850, commenced practice Aberdeen: 1856), 86

F

Fairlie, Dr Reginald, 87, 94, 139

Fairley, James Graham (1846-1934: app. Thornton Shiells; dr. Major du Cane, London: commenced practice Dundee, 1877-1879), 48, 95

Fairweather, John, 55

Findlater, James Rattray (c. 1803-1873: commenced practice Dundee 1832)

Freeman and Ogilvy, 103, 122

Friskin, William Wallace (app. Campbell R. Hislop, Glasgow), 86, 94, 119

Fulton, John (d. 1882: Burgh Engineer: emigrated to Texas 1868)

Index to Buildings

RIAS/Landmark

Architectural Guides to Scotland

Edinburgh: An illustrated architectural guide. £3.50. "One of the best guides to any city in the United Kingdom." — *The Architects Journal.*

Dundee: An illustrated introduction through its buildings. £3.95.

Stirling and District: An illustrated introduction through its buildings. £3.95. (Autumn 1984.)

Titles in preparation
Aberdeen
Perth
Scottish Architecture 1930-40

Other architectural books
Scotstyle: an examination of the last 150 years of Scots architecture. £7.50 (paper). £12.00 (board). Author: Fiona Sinclair.

Published in association with
The Scottish Academic Press
33 Montgomery Street
Edinburgh

All available from
The RIAS Bookshop
15 Rutland Square, Edinburgh EH1 2BE